D1490963

EVERY CHILD IS A WINNER

EVERY CHILD IS A WINNER

DEVELOPING CONFIDENCE THAT LASTS A LIFETIME

Caz McCaslin and Bobb Biehl

President of Upward Unlimited

President of Masterplanning Group International

—————— *with* ——————

LINDA JEFFORDS GILDEN

BROADMAN
&HOLMAN
PUBLISHERS

NASHVILLE, TENNESSEE

0-8054-2569-1

Published by Broadman & Holman Publishers,
Nashville, Tennessee

Subject Heading: PARENTING

Unless otherwise stated all Scripture citation is from the Holy
Bible, New International Version, © 1973, 1978, 1984 by
International Bible Society.

1 2 3 4 5 6 7 8 9 10 06 05 04 03 02

To my wife, Leslie

After my salvation, she is the greatest gift the Lord has ever given me. She never ceases to amaze me with her unfailing love and support of what God has called us to do in ministry. And, with her parenting wisdom, Leslie truly has taught me many wonderful ways to draw out the winners in our children.

I also dedicate this book to our three girls:

Lauren, Keighlee, and Mari Caroline

ALL winners!

—Caz McCaslin

Contents

Acknowledgments

I am so grateful that I have this opportunity to acknowledge a few of the very special people who have made significant contributions to the writing of this book.

My appreciation goes out to the Upward Unlimited Board of Directors for the freedom they have given me to write this book. Each of you has brought to the table unique gifts and abilities that have made an impact on my life. I covet your prayers and endless support.

Thank you, Gary Terashita, for your encouragement to finish the task at hand. You are a tremendous motivator. Also, I must acknowledge the Recreation Department at LifeWay Christian Resources, especially John Garner. You were there from the beginning to launch Upward Basketball and have been a loyal supporter of our ministry ever since. I appreciate you.

Lastly, my heartfelt appreciation must be reserved for my writer, Linda Gilden. You have done a beautiful job over the past year of interpreting my words to express what is in my heart. Thanks for all of your hard work and countless hours of revisions. I can't think of anyone else that I would have enjoyed working with as much. Without you, this book would not have been possible. You are simply the best!

Introduction

Have you ever gone to a youth basketball, baseball, or soccer game and, after watching for only a short time, picked out the kids that have what it takes? Even on the playground you can pick out the children who have that spark—the intensity, the competitive spirit, the desire to make it. You can simply look at them and tell that they have "it."

But then a lot of people might say, "You don't understand. My child's not a star; he's not a winner. He doesn't have what it takes. Sure, he's a great kid, but that's it—he's *just* an average kid, not a *winner.*"

I can't tell you how many times I have heard that.

Nowadays children are started in sports earlier and earlier. There are soccer teams for three-year-olds, basketball teams for four-year-olds, and hockey teams for three-year-olds. Parents usually put their children into organized sports because they see the value of team participation, but now they are starting them earlier because they want their children to catch the drive and the passion of the game.

This spawns all kinds of unfortunate situations. As the competition gets more and more intense, everyone gets more and more emotionally involved in the games. Then by their early teens, when children begin making their own decisions about which activities to be involved in, they drop out.

According to Barna Research Group, one of the main things children dislike about sports is the way their parents react when they watch them play. Children also don't like the way coaches stress winning as the most important thing—"You've got to win and you have to win at all costs." Coaches have all kinds of stipulations that children must do to contribute to the team.

As a result, 75 percent of all children who play a sport drop out by the time they are thirteen. Are all these kids failures just because they never had the experience of being on a championship team? Just because a child doesn't win a ball game or a championship, does he wake up in the morning and say, "I must be a loser"?

Have you ever seen the movie *The Kid?* It tells an incredible story. It is about a forty-year-old man who goes through life and suddenly bumps into his eight-year-old self. Now think about that. He's eight, about the same age that children are involved in group sports. For some reason, the movie's producers decided to bring the man back to this moment in his life. Seeing himself at age eight causes the man to look back on all of the things in life that made him turn out the way that he is.

He wonders, *Why does my eye twitch? Why am I angry so often? Why do I cut people off?* Essentially he tries to pinpoint why, in his own mind, he's a loser.

The eight-year-old version of himself discovers that he never achieved the things that had been important to him at eight: the man is not married, he's afraid of commitment, he doesn't have a dog, and he's not able to fly planes. All of those things were so much a part of his eight-year-old life.

For some reason, the man spent the rest of his life trying to forget them. He tried to become a winner by stepping on top of other people and making them seem lower than himself.

At the end of the movie, the man not only has to deal with the eight-year-old version of who he is, but he has an encounter with a sixty-year-old future version of who he is going to become. In fact, the sixty-year-old version is now married, has his dream dog, and is the pilot of his own airplane.

The end of that movie had one of the strongest impacts on me of any I have ever seen. After watching his sixty-year-old self fly off with wife and dog in his own plane, the forty-year-old man raises his hands to the air and screams out as though to God, "I'm not a loser!"

He looks back to tell the eight-year-old boy the same thing, but he's gone. So he looks back to the plane and the airport, but the planes are gone. For the first time in his life, at age forty, the man realizes he is not a loser. He is a *winner*. And it has nothing to do with winning or losing.

Unfortunately, many of our children today don't realize they are not losers until they are forty years old or older. The reason is because they had to discover it by themselves. But it doesn't have to be that way. As parents, coaches, teachers—we have the opportunity to let impressionable children know that *every child is a winner!*

What Is Winning?

What is a winner? What is winning? What is winning all about?

Whether applied to my family life or to Upward Basketball, the definition I like best is this: Winning is learning and/or teaching lessons in the game of life. If you're learning yourself or teaching someone else how to manage the ins and outs of living, you are a winner. Specifically, there are three main characteristics that contribute to being a winner: salvation, character, and self-esteem.

Salvation

God loves each one of us and has a plan for our lives. In fact, He created us because He wants fellowship with us. Now, would He create us for fellowship and then make us losers? Of course not. But still we know that we fall short and make mistakes in life, separating ourselves from God. Thankfully, it doesn't have to end there. God made sure there was a plan to get us back into fellowship. If we reconcile with God, we're winners once again. If we can accept that truth and teach it, we are not only winners ourselves; we can draw the winner out of our children.

Character

The second characteristic of a winner is character. Character in a child is honesty, purity, kindness, respect, commitment, involvement; the list could go on and on. But the best trait of character is being a servant. Think about the people whom you know that have the biggest impact on you; they are probably people with character, integrity, and a servant's heart. Those people are winners.

Self-Esteem

The third characteristic is self-esteem. It is nearly impossible to accomplish anything in the world if you look in the mirror and miss the incredible creation you are! Step 1 is knowing *you* are a winner. From the moment you were conceived, God and a lot of people have had to go to a lot of trouble to keep you alive. It is worth it all because you are a winner!

Every Child IS a Winner

Inside every child is the opportunity for salvation, character, and self-esteem; therefore, every child is a winner. If you consistently teach these three things to your children and those children around you, you are going to be surrounded by winners. And not only are these characteristics teachable; they are free!

If a child is learning or teaching life lessons, that child is a winner. She may play basketball; he may be a football or soccer player; she may swim or play tennis; he may play the piano or be an artist. Although all of these activities are great, there are a lot of other things that make every child a winner. It's not contingent on accomplishing the highest mark in any one activity.

The title of this book is *Every Child* IS *a Winner.* We emphasize the word *is* not because every child *might* be a winner, or every child *could* be a winner, or every child *has the potential* to be a winner. Every child already *is* a winner. They already are because *God made them that way.*

Many times I have been in a gym or on a soccer field in a competitive athletic situation and have heard parents or coaches say, "Man, that kid's got it. You can just see the desire in him. He stands out among all the others. Now there's a winner."

Is athletic prowess the only quality you need to be a winner? Sadly, I have seen some of the most gifted athletes in the world in our local prisons. I hope athleticism is not our only measuring stick.

What about a child who is born with a birth defect? I once knew a child named Kevin. The doctors didn't expect Kevin to live past two or three months of age, yet he lived for seven years. Throughout those seven years Kevin lived in a crib—unable to speak, unable to talk, unable to respond. Kevin just lay there.

He had brothers and sisters in his family along with his mom and dad, and all of them absolutely, positively loved Kevin. They understood from a very unique perspective what unconditional love was. They came in and loved Kevin and expected nothing in return. Those brothers and sisters took care of him and didn't expect some sort of payback. As they looked at and talked to their disabled brother, they often left, went outside to play, and many times came back with a renewed realization of what they had.

Kevin lived in a crib. Did he ever win a ball game, make an *A* on a test, or play a song on the piano? Did he ever learn anything about the lessons in life? No, but does that make him a loser? Or could it be that Kevin was *teaching* lessons just by being himself on this earth? He taught many lessons to his mom and dad. Kevin taught many lessons to his brothers and sisters, as well as everybody else that came in contact with him. God used Kevin to teach lessons to a lot of people. If you were to ask his brothers and sisters who was the greatest winner in their family, they would say Kevin. If it hadn't been for him, they would have never realized how fortunate and blessed they were. They wouldn't have realized how God had used Kevin to teach them about love, compassion, service, caring, and family unity. God used Kevin to teach others about things that are often taken for granted.

Kevin is a winner to God. He's a winner because he taught lessons in the game of life. He taught by just being who he was, who God created him to be. I'm sure that everybody in Kevin's family and everybody that knew him grew in character. I'm sure their self-esteem went up too. And I wouldn't be surprised if somehow through the life that Kevin lived there were some who came to understand salvation. In every characteristic of winning, Kevin was a winner—maybe not from learning but from teaching. And that's what made the difference.

CHAPTER 1

What Do You Want for Your Children?

Not too long ago I spoke at a church in Florida, a big, old church that does Upward Basketball. When they invited me to come, they asked if I would speak to all of the parents of Upward Basketball players. I said, "Yes, I would love to."

About two weeks later they called me back and said, "Caz, we still want you to come down and speak, but we want you to speak to the kids, not the parents."

I said, "I appreciate you telling me because the preparation is different. When you talk to kids, it is from one direction; when you talk to parents, it is from another."

Well, when I got down there, they said, "OK, we are going in the dining room now, and this is where all of the parents and all of the kids are going to be. We need you to speak to them all at the same time."

I had misunderstood! Although it was exciting to have the opportunity to speak to both groups, that was not the program for which I had prepared. Quickly I made an adjustment in what I was going to do.

I decided to test a philosophy that I had had in mind for a long time. I thought, *Well, here we are live and in person. It's time to find out if my philosophy about what parents want for their children and what children want is correct.*

First, I addressed all of the kids. "I want to talk to the kids right now. I don't want anybody else to respond, just children."

I got a dry erase board and a marker, and I said, "Boys and girls, I want you to tell me something you want. It doesn't matter how wild or expensive or crazy it is. Tell me something that you'd like for Christmas or your birthday, whatever the case may be. I want you to tell me something you want."

Immediately, they started throwing out all kinds of answers.

"I want a puppy dog!"

"I want a doll baby!"

"I want a Nintendo 64!"

"A go-cart!"

"I want a new bicycle!"

"A kitty cat!"

The list went on and on. I could hardly write the answers down fast enough.

"I want a new violin!"

"I want an American Girl doll!"

"A basketball!"

"I want a baseball glove!"

"A soccer ball!"

There wasn't even a pause; I was pointing to kids left and right. One child said, "I want five hundred dollars!"

It was almost comical listening to the things they were throwing out. When they finally ran out of things to say and I had finished writing them all down, I said, "OK, boys and girls, I don't want you to say a single word now. This time I'm talking to your moms and dads. Just parents.

"Now, what I would like for you to do, Moms and Dads, is not tell me what you want, but tell me what you want *for your kids*. What do you want *for your child?* We just listed all of the things your children wanted. Now tell me what you want for them."

After some serious thought and a few quiet moments, I said, "Come on, can anybody tell me what they want for their children?"

Finally somebody raised their hand and said, "Salvation."

I thought, *Man, now that's great.*

The parents continued. "Faith!"

"Integrity!"

"Character!"

I wrote as fast as they called things out.

"Confidence!"

"Humility!"

Are you with me? I don't think there was one person in the group yelling for "go-carts"!

They continued.

"Self-esteem!"

"Wisdom!"

Every one of these things—and more—was mentioned. I looked down at my list and realized that the philosophy I had had in my mind for so long had proved true: Children, regardless of how old they are (sometimes they can be forty!), really want something they can hang on to. "I'm going to see how many toys I can gather up, how many things I can put in my pocket." The older they get, the bigger the stuff gets. "Man, I want a bigger house; I want a bigger car; I want to make more money. I want a beach house; I want a lake house. . . ."

I'm not saying there is anything wrong with any of these things. What I am saying is that as children we begin to gather up things that we want, trying to see how much we can collect.

The moment we became parents, however, it's not *stuff* that we want for our children. We want them to have the things that can't be touched, the things that are unseen.

What we want for our children is the same as what God wants for us, His children. Second Corinthians 4:18 says, "We fix our eyes not on what is seen, but on what is unseen. For what is seen is temporary, but what is unseen is eternal."

The things God really wants for us are the same things parents desire for their children, the things in life that matter: character, wisdom, and self-esteem. I also believe that if parents are truly honest with themselves, they also want their children to go to heaven. They want eternal life for their children, even if they don't understand what eternal life is.

The more I watch my own children, the more I realize they are a reflection of who I am. It doesn't matter how hard I try to *tell* them what I want them to be; what they see every day is what will influence their character, raise their self-esteem, or lead them to salvation. Conversely, if they observe a lust for more stuff, their desire will be raised for the same. It is important for me to realize that they are becoming more of who I am every day. Therefore, who *I* am makes a big difference.

The truth is, if we focus on and desire the unseen things for ourselves, that desire will overflow to our kids. It will help to draw out the winner that is in all our children. Teaching life lessons—that's what makes a winner. Scoring points and winning championships are not the important things. What is important is understanding what it takes to win at the game of life—salvation, character, and self-esteem.

CHAPTER 2

What Would You Do to Get These Things?

We have established some of the things parents want for their children, and salvation, character, and self-esteem top the list. These things are not easily imparted, however. In order to instill salvation, character, and self-esteem in our children, we must be prepared to take advantage of every teachable moment.

The next big question that comes into play is, What would you do as a parent to get these things for your children? What would you do to be sure that your child would receive a spot in heaven? What would you do to be sure that the child you hold in your arms, the life that you have the privilege of raising, has the opportunity to have these things?

Upward Basketball uses a basketball as a tool to share the Lord with children. We use it as a tool to help raise their character. We use it as a tool to build self-esteem. But it's just one tool of many that you can use as a parent.

There's a Chinese proverb that says, "If you want to prosper for a year, then grow grain. If you want to prosper for ten years, then grow trees. But if you want to prosper for one hundred years, then grow people."

Gary O'Sullivan is a dear friend. He once said to me, "Principles never change; only techniques and application do." You can take any principle that you have seen work, and you can apply it to many different circumstances.

We have come up with an Upward proverb that is a takeoff of that Chinese proverb. It goes like this: "If you want to make an impact on a child for a year, then teach him to play a game. If you want to make an impact on a child for one hundred years, then teach that child how to read and memorize Scripture. But if you want to impact a child for eternity, then share the love of Jesus Christ with that child."

CHAPTER 3
Be Prepared

*W*hen the opportunity arises, it is too late to prepare.

In my life as a parent, as well as in many other areas, this statement has proven true over and over again. I can even look back to my childhood and recognize many situations when this principle rang true. If I had just listened to my parents . . . . Or, as a parent, if I had just stood my ground a little firmer on some issues . . . . The fact of the matter is, however, *when the opportunity arises, it's too late to prepare.*

There are going to be many times when you have an opportunity to impact a child. That child will then have the opportunity to make a right or wrong decision. Many opportunities are going to come your way, but they remain mere opportunities until you turn them into teachable moments. Therefore you must be prepared for every situation, remembering that when opportunities arise, it's too late to prepare.

Of course, it's never too late to build a child's self-esteem, but he or she must be prepared before the moment it is needed. Children don't just wake up one day and have self-esteem. It's a process. Unfortunately when children get to junior high school, it's hard to build their self-esteem. Then when they are faced with opposition to integrity and character, it's too late to prepare them—at least for that moment. You must help children develop confidence before they get there.

Decisions made when nobody else is watching are decisions based on personal integrity and character. That integrity and character is something that has been built from years of nurturing from one situation or another. You've either got that character and integrity or you don't. That is why children and teenagers need the opportunity to prepare for the moment when they are faced with temptations and tough character decisions.

In 1 Corinthians 10:13, the Bible tells us that "no temptation has seized you except what is common to man. And God is faithful; he will not let you be tempted beyond what you can bear. But when you are tempted, he will also provide a way out so that you can stand up under it."

Think of it this way. Catherine walks into a room and sees that it is a place where she doesn't need to be. The door that Catherine came through is wide open. If she looks in and says, "I am not supposed to be here," she can turn around and walk right back out the door and that will be the end of it. That's exactly what Paul was talking about when he said, "God is faithful and will never let you be tempted beyond that which you can bear."

Unfortunately, we sometimes try to push that Scripture to the limit. We flirt with temptation until the way of escape becomes very small.

The following story that I told my own daughter may help illustrate this danger.

Lauren, when you begin making decisions about who you are going to date, there is one very important fact: You have already made the decision that you want to be pure and righteous before God when you get married. You don't want to have sex before your wedding day because you want to give your purity to your husband out of love for him and obedience to God's Word.

Now, suppose there's this guy at school who happens to be the high school quarterback—a real "stud muffin." He is good looking, popular, and some kind of athlete. He's the total package. The only downside is that part of his resumé is a bad reputation. Everybody knows it. On the other hand, your reputation is to stay pure.

This quarterback calls you and says, "I'd like to go out on a date with you on Friday night."

You now have a decision to make. You're standing "inside the room" with this guy, and the door is wide open. You can turn around and see that wide-open door and say this is not what you need to do. You can walk out the door by telling the guy, "No, I don't think this is a good idea, but thank you."

Or, you can tell yourself that just because you go out on a date with him doesn't mean you're going to have sex with him. So you say, "Sure I can go out on a date. That would be great." You feel proud because you have a date with the school's best-looking guy, the quarterback, the stud dog. Friday night after the game, it will be you and him having pizza out there in front of everybody.

Well, let me tell you what happens the moment you say yes. That door starts to close about halfway.

Is there still a way to escape? Yes, there sure is. Absolutely. But when that door closes halfway, you are there—already "in the room" with him. You are walking down a path where you don't want to be.

So, he picks you up and says, "Would you like to go get some pizza, or would you like to go to my house and order in? My mom and dad aren't home!"

At that moment the door is half open. You can still get out the door by saying, "Why don't we just go get pizza?"

Or you can say, "That's fine. Whatever you want to do." And he says, "That's great; let's go to my house." All of a sudden, you are on your way to his house, where it will be only you and him. That door now closes all but shut.

Once you get to his house, there's nothing but a crack in the door. That way of escape that God promises is still there, but it is very difficult to find. You must say right then, "We have to go."

I'm going to tell you something: it's a whole lot harder to get out that door when it's only cracked than when it is wide open. So what's my point? When that opportunity arises, it's too late to prepare. You must make decisions *today*, in broad daylight, way before the circumstance comes up. Are you going to turn around and walk through that wide-open door, or are you going to hang out in there until there is nothing but a crack left for escape?

When the pizza man is gone, the door is closed. It is too late. You have already put yourself in a situation where you are not going to be able to back out. And at that point, it is *too late to prepare.*

As adults, we need to understand the decision process young people go through and help them see that it is much easier to make them *now—before* they ever get in tempting situations. We must prepare them before the opportunity to become involved arises.

Will your children have sex before marriage? Will they drink alcohol? Will they ride in a car with someone who has been drinking? Will they drive while drunk?

As a parent, what would you do to be sure that your children have the salvation, character, and self-esteem necessary to make these kinds of decisions? I believe your answer is the same as mine—"I'll do whatever it takes—absolutely, positively, beyond a shadow of a doubt, *whatever it takes* to make sure they make good choices." I would give anything for my three daughters to understand today the things that I now understand after living through those same circumstances.

Ask yourself, "Do I want the things that are unseen more than the things that are seen for my child?" I'm sure you do. Sometimes, however—whether it is because of a bad day at work, problems at home, or the distractions of life—we, as adults, walk in and out of our children's changing lives and let the door close right behind us. We let teachable opportunities go by almost every day.

My children are not perfect, and neither am I. I know I have missed many opportunities and will probably miss some more. But I want to do whatever it takes to bring out the winner in my child. Don't you?

CHAPTER 4

Whatever It Takes

The greatest whatever-it-takes story that I've ever heard is the story of Dr. Johnny Hunt. It literally changed the direction of my life.

When I served on staff at a church, I was there for ten years. One of the programs we had there was Upward Basketball. Our desire was to have a ministry through basketball, so we started a league. The first year it was very ministry oriented, with about 150 players. It kept growing until we had about 520 children involved. Our gym was slam full of first through sixth graders. We thought we had done all we could do, and, honestly, I began to get a little prideful.

The following year we sent out our registration brochures, and in three days we had 520 children registered and twenty-seven children on a waiting list. I'll never forget it. It was probably one of the proudest moments I have ever had— as far as accomplishment is concerned. We had built the program from nothing, and now we were turning kids away.

Looking back at that moment, I am disappointed in myself. I went home that day and told my wife, "Sweetheart, we have got the most happening league in all of Spartanburg, South Carolina. Five hundred and twenty children and twenty-seven kids on the waiting list! We are completely full!"

She said, "Honey, if what you want to do is have twenty-seven kids on a waiting list, then I'm proud of you."

I said, "Wait, wait, wait, honey. You missed it!"

She said, "What? If what you want is to turn children away, then you did well."

I figured that she didn't realize what she was saying. It didn't even register with her that we had 520 kids. While I was bloated up and pretty happy about all the kids we did have, she was concerned about the twenty-seven we had to say no to. If there is anything that my wife hates to do, it's to say no. She doesn't like to turn people away from something she knows they will enjoy. I shrugged it off and started planning our season. I told everybody in town about our 520 kids and how great it was going to be.

Also during this time our church ministerial staff had a meeting of all the leaders and spouses in our church. We came together in our dining hall—more than six hundred of us—for the sole purpose of learning how we were going to continue to grow our church. For about four or five years, our church's attendance had begun to plateau.

A pastor, Dr. Johnny Hunt, had been invited to speak to those of us who were responsible for helping to grow the church. I wasn't sure we needed someone from the "outside" telling us what to do. We had all kinds of activities going on at the church. I thought, *Who is this guy to come in and tell us how to grow our church? We're doing fine.* I sat there with my arms crossed, wondering what in the world he was going to say.

When our minister of education stood up to introduce the speaker, he said, "I want to share with you a little bit about Dr. Johnny Hunt." His credentials were astounding. When he was called to the church in Woodstock, Georgia, they had about four hundred members, an average attendance of about two hundred members, and a sanctuary that seated six hundred people. Dr. Hunt led his people to do whatever it takes to reach lost people. Fourteen years later, that church was in the process of building a 7,200-seat auditorium—and would still need to have two services. They were growing like crazy. Woodstock was a booming area—and it looked like people were moving there just to go to church!

Dr. Johnny Hunt's credentials got my attention. When he stood up to speak, I was ready to listen!

The first thing out of his mouth was, "Before I can say anything to you folks, you've got to understand a few things. I have never been to your church before. I don't have any idea of what kind of educational space you have. I don't know if you have a choir or youth group or singles' department or anything else. I just drove here from Atlanta, got out of my car, and here I am. I'm going to share with you what God has laid on my heart, and then I'm going to get in my car and drive home. So a lot of you are probably sitting here thinking, *Who are you to tell us how to grow our church?*"

There I sat—guilty as charged!

He continued, "Before I can share anything with you, I need to know something: Why is it that you have a preschool ministry? Why do you have a children's ministry? Why do you have a youth ministry? Why do you have a singles' ministry? Why do you have a choir? For that matter, why do you have a pastor who stands up at the pulpit every Sunday morning and preaches from the Bible? Why do you have these things in your church? I just need to know."

People all over the room began to answer, but nothing was more resounding than a man who stood up and said, "To share the love of Jesus Christ with those who don't know Him."

Dr. Hunt said, "Is there anybody here who can give me a better answer than that one right there?" Silence. Beautiful, committed silence. All it took was a little bit of time to focus on why we do what we do.

Well, nobody in our church could come up with a better answer than sharing Christ. Nobody wanted to try. We existed to share the love of God with those who didn't know Him. That was an incredible realization for us.

Then he said, "If that's the case, then if you've got a Sunday school class in this church that is 80 percent full, you've got to begin preparing right now for when you get to 90 percent. Eventually, people are going to walk through that door, see a full room, and walk out. They will talk about it, feel very uncomfortable, and then they are going to go home. The bottom line is, if you are turning away people from this church or any part of it, you are turning away the opportunity to share Christ with those people."

Dr. Hunt developed that point for the next thirty-five minutes. Then he pointed his finger at the crowd (it seemed as though he pointed directly at me) and closed with this statement: "If you've something as simple as a gym in this church and you are turning kids away from playing basketball, then you might as well stick a yellow flashing sign in front of your gym door that says, 'Go to hell. We're full.'"

That statement changed my life. Full of emotion, I got up out of my seat and ran to my car. My wife came right behind me, sat down beside me, put her arms around me, and said, "Honey, what are you going to do?"

All I could say was, "Whatever it takes."

CHAPTER 5
What's Your Burden?

Once, on the way home from vacation, I asked my children their definition of a burden. This is what my fourteen-, twelve-, and eight-year-olds agreed on: "A burden is something you want really, really badly, and you'll do anything to get it. But you can't hold it in your hands or put it in your pocket." I like their definition.

When Dr. Hunt pointed his finger at me, a burden was created in my heart. That burden was for lost kids and their families. I suddenly knew the focus of my ministry at my church and in my home.

When you have a burden, it does a lot of things for you.

In his book *The 21 Most Powerful Minutes in a Leader's Day*, John Maxwell states three specific things a burden does: it purifies motives, cultivates persistence, and cements your convictions.

A Burden Purifies Motives

Think about that for a second. A burden purifies your motives. If you have a true burden, that burden always benefits others. When you have a burden within you to accomplish something, it is very difficult to be selfish.

I can't help but use the example of sports. When I see adults (coaches and parents) overreacting, I wonder what their "burden" is. If they have the desire to win a ball game at all costs, that is nothing but selfishness and something they want to accomplish for themselves. That's want *they* want. As a result, everybody suffers.

But if the coach's and parent's burden is to make the game a positive experience for a child, then it's impossible to have a selfish motive. That burden is going to purify the adult's motive.

As a parent, if your burden is to draw out the winner in your child, one of the quickest things that happens is that you stop thinking about yourself and start thinking about the child. The minute a woman gets pregnant, doesn't she stop thinking about what she wants and start thinking, *What do I have to do to get ready for this child? What kind of car do I need to drive for my child? What kind of doorknobs do I need to put on my door so my child doesn't have access to something harmful?*

Immediately, the mom-to-be starts thinking about something completely different from what *she* wants; she thinks about what she wants for her child. She wants safety for her child. Even the conversation she has with her husband differs from what it was before. It was, "Where do we want to go on vacation? What do we want to do this summer? Where do we want to go skiing?" Now it becomes, "I wonder how many times we will go home to see Grandma? I wonder how many times she'll come up here? Have we got a place for Mom and Dad to come and stay with the kids?" You start thinking completely differently once you become a parent. That is what a burden does. It purifies your motives.

A Burden Cultivates Persistence

It stimulates persistence in who you are and what you are doing. Cultivating persistence means that there are things about carrying this burden that are going to be tough. It's not going to be easy.

We have opportunities to do many great things in this world; but when you have a burden, you are going to have the persistence not to quit. When it comes to priority, burdens go straight to the top. We may quit playing tennis or golf or singing in the choir, but we need to adamantly say, "We will not give up on my kids."

There are a lot of moms and dads out there who have made complete life-changing decisions because they decided their children are more important than the *original* schedule in their lives. That's persistence. That's why moms don't quit. That's why dads don't quit. If you have the burden to make sure your child is a winner, you are going to have the persistence not to give up. There are going to be times when that child does something, and you will ask yourself, "Why is he doing this? Why is she doing this? I'm just going to throw in the towel." But you can't throw the towel in on your own child. You can't throw the towel in on something that God created. That is what a burden does. You won't quit.

A Burden Cements Your Convictions

Convictions mean you are going to choose to do one thing, as opposed to doing something of lesser value. The burden we are stressing here is making sure that your child is a winner. This means putting aside the things that might selfishly be the things *you* want to do. You are more concerned now with your child than you are with the things that you would have done in your own life. Your focus is different.

One of the biggest questions we must ask ourselves as we approach parenthood, coaching, teaching, or any activity that presents an opportunity to impact a child is: Do you see *yourself* as a winner? Before you can try to draw out the winner in a child, you must realize that you, too, are a child of God. God created *you* a winner. It's like that movie, *The Kid*, that we talked about in the very beginning. The man didn't know he was a winner until he was forty. There might be somebody reading this book right now who is saying, "You don't understand; my child can't be a winner because I'm a loser." If you're thinking that about yourself, you must realize that this is not the case. God created you a winner, and it's time to let it surface.

Before you can understand children, you must first understand yourself. It is necessary to first understand why God created you to be who you are and then to do the things He has asked you to do.

CHAPTER 6
Good Habits for Life

When I was a child I pouted whenever I lost a ball game. I became very upset with myself, and it ruined my day. I wanted to win every single game. My self-worth was based on winning or losing, and my attitude changes after each game were based on the results of the game.

Realizing how intense I was, my dad came to me one day and said, "Remember last year when you played the Tigers?"

I said, "Well, I kind of remember," even though I didn't really.

"Did you win that game?"

"Well, I don't remember."

"Exactly," Dad said. "Merely winning or losing doesn't matter in the long run. But if you will just *learn* something from this game, you are a winner no matter what the outcome of the game is."

I recently had an opportunity to speak at a high school baseball breakfast in my hometown. Before

I went, I looked on the Internet and found the names of the last fifteen most valuable players in major league baseball, the last fifteen teams that won the World Series, and the guy who has had the highest batting average ever. There were some pretty incredible statistics.

At the breakfast, I sat in front of several high school juniors and seniors who were aspiring to play baseball professionally, boys who *love* the game. Yet no one in that room could name the most valuable player beyond more than two years back. Nobody could tell me who won the World Series more than three years back (and all three years it was the Yankees!). These teens thought baseball was something so incredible that they poured *all* their time into it, but in reality, it is temporary at *any* level.

Then I asked them, "Why do we have Easter?"

"Well, that's the day when we celebrate Jesus Christ raised from the dead."

"What's Christmas?"

"Well, that's the day that Jesus was born."

They were right. Both events happened two thousand years ago. So, how do they remember that? It's because those things are *eternal*, not temporary. Second Corinthians 4:18 says, "So we fix our eyes not on what is seen, but on what is unseen. For what is seen is temporary, but what is unseen is eternal." To draw out the winner in someone, focus on the unseen!

When I look back on those games when I pouted and the things my dad told me, I realize I learned a lesson—a lesson in life. Because of that, I was a winner. You don't have to win the ball game to be a winner; you just have to *learn something* from that ball game.

Not too long ago I was at a conference on leadership. The conference was about setting life goals *and* meeting them. At this conference there was one word I had never heard. The word is *engram*. An *engram* is a thought process that through repetition or emotional contact can move through your head at the speed of light, and it moves faster and faster with more repetition. Great! What does that mean?

When you were learning to ride a bicycle, you probably had somebody holding the bicycle as you climbed on. Your helper told you where to put your feet on the pedals and steadied the handlebar and the back of the seat. This person even ran along beside you as you learned to balance.

My youngest daughter, Mari Caroline, just experienced this. At first she would hang on so tightly that her knuckles were white. Her feet were on the pedals, but she was shaking so badly that she wobbled back and forth. She was holding on tightly and pedaling and thinking about every movement of the wheel. She was so stiff and timid because she was afraid she might forget to do some part of the process and fall down.

As she continued to learn this new task, she got to the point where I could let go and she would continue to ride. But it didn't change her rigidness—yet. Every day we practiced; however, there were different parts of riding that bicycle she didn't have to think about. First it was hopping on the bicycle; then, lining up her pedals; then, grabbing the handlebars; then, taking the first couple of pedals. Finally, she was just working on balancing.

After much practice, she stopped gripping so tightly. She got on the bicycle, lined up her pedals, and off she went. Now when we come home, she picks up her bike, jumps on, and is gone.

With practice, riding her bicycle became a new engram for Mari Caroline. Our brain develops engrams because the more we repeat a process, the more natural it becomes. Even though each time we ride a bicycle our minds have to go through the exact same process as it did the very first time, the difference is that the process happens so fast that we don't have to think about it. Unlike man-made computers that process information at a set rate, the more information and repetitiveness you give your mind, the faster it goes. It moves at the speed of light.

Every single day we do things that we once had to think about and process, things that once required quite a bit of thought: driving a car, using a computer, hitting the brakes, putting the gearshift in park. Yet we don't even think about these things anymore because we have done them so many times. How many times did you turn your blinker on the last time you went to the grocery store? You have no idea. How many times did you turn left? Turn right? Those are things that are processed so quickly in your mind that they have become a natural part of your life. They have become engrams.

We need to create engrams for ourselves and for our children because the right engrams help draw out the winner in each of us. The engrams created in our lives affect who we are, the decisions we make, and what we do. Therefore, who we become is based on the engrams we decide to create from this point forward in our own lives and in the lives of our children.

Sometimes those engrams involve decision-making processes. For example, whatever you have to do that you put off until later, just decide to do it right the first time. You will be surprised how effective you can be when you create the engram to "do it right the first time." Mow the yard; wash the car; process mail—what a daily impact that would have on your children.

You may decide that you want your children to wake up every day and make their beds. The first few weeks it is hard for them to remember. They might even complain. It may not be so neat. But day after day of practice soon creates an engram. They will make their beds so well that they will do it *before* they wake up.

To bring out the winner in your children, help them create engrams that will set them up to succeed. And while you are at it, create a few for yourself. Exercise four times a week; eat breakfast every day; tell your loved ones how much you love them; do something special for your spouse weekly; read your Bible every day; talk to God continuously. Create an engram! Bring out the winner!

CHAPTER 7
Four Levels of Thinking

A s we help our children create engrams, our goal should be to help them confidently understand, "It's OK to be me, the me God created me to be." To accomplish this, we must guide them through the four levels of thinking. Our children may not be the same kind of winners we are, but they are winners nonetheless.

I have some dear friends who have played professional sports. In the beginning, they looked at their children and thought, *Someday, these children are going to be in the big leagues.* But in talking with them on different occasions, they have said to me that based on what they have seen, their children may not make it in the big leagues.

Does that make their children any less winners just because they aren't going to play major league baseball or play in the NBA? Absolutely not. Each of us has different types of abilities, different types of gifts that God has given to make us winners. It doesn't have to be athletics. It may be music. It may be art. It may be accounting. Whatever the case, we are all winners!

In order to grasp the idea that we really are winners, we must reach an understanding of just *who* we are. As we strive to come to that realization, we usually go through four levels of thinking about ourselves: (1) Everyone is like me; (2) Everyone is not like me; (3) Nobody is like me; (4) It's OK to be me—the me God made me to be.

Level 1: Everyone Is Like Me

"Everyone is like me. We are all the same. Everybody likes what I like, and everybody wants what I want because everybody in the world is just like me. That's just the way it is."

Level 2: Everyone Is Not Like Me

"Everyone is not just like me. There are some people who actually like accounting or the color orange. Not everybody's like me. I don't like accounting. Orange is not my favorite color. I can't imagine it, but there are people who are not like me."

Level 3: Nobody Is Like Me

"Nobody's like me. I am completely unique. I have different parents, go to different schools, have different interests—there is nobody exactly like me." The question at this level is, will this be a good thing or a bad thing? It's a self-esteem issue. Think about this from a child's perspective. This level is very real in junior high school, but the crucial question is how to deal with it. Does a child at that age want to be unique or just like everyone else? It's important to get to level 4.

Nobody is like me and . . .

Level 4: It's OK to Be Me— the Me God Made Me to Be

"I don't look like others. I don't act like others. And it's OK. I like me."

This is the final step.

Moving through these levels often happens way too slowly. Some people never get to level 4. Some people get stuck in the "no one is like me" level, and their self-esteem goes completely down the tubes because they really feel like they should be like everyone else.

As I have watched my three daughters grow up, I have seen each of them realize these levels at different times. "Hey, everybody's like me." It didn't matter if the person was red or yellow, black or white; whether they sat in a wheelchair or a nursing home bed; whether they spoke by sign language or couldn't talk at all. My girls would walk up to anybody, anytime, anywhere, and hug on them and love on them because they thought, *Everybody's like me.*

The older they got, however, the smarter they got. Next they realized, "That guy's a different color than I am. That person is taller than me. That person is skinnier than me. That person doesn't walk like me; she rolls around in a chair all the time."

After some time at that level they realized, "Hey, there is nobody like me." This level was usually reached later in elementary school or even junior high school. This is a time when, unfortunately, some of our children want to back up and be like everybody else. "I want to be what they are." Instead of going to the next level and saying, "You know what? It's OK to be me. This is who I am supposed to be. I am supposed to be different. I don't have to be like everybody else," their self-esteem gets hung up in level 3. They look for acceptance from others rather than seeing the uniqueness of the gifts God has given them.

The key is to understand the different levels of thinking in a positive light and strive to get to level 4. Then you start developing the groundwork for drawing out the winner in your child. But before you can ever do that for your children, you have to find out where *you* are. Ask yourself, "What level am I on today?" If you understand your burden, your passion, and your level of thinking, positive things begin to happen just because you have that focus.

One dad had his son involved in a city basketball league, and the boy wasn't getting much playing time. There were a lot of things going on that were unfair to the normal, average child. Like a lot of leagues, the only children who got to play were the star athletes. Everybody else played the minimum time, a few minutes here or a few minutes there, and were really not treated very much like part of the team. They had to come to all of the practices, but they ended up sitting on the bench most of the time.

This dad decided to bring his child to play Upward Basketball. It didn't take too long to realize that this particular dad was pretty intense at games and could be a little hard on the referees. When the first game rolled around, the man came expecting great things because the rules were that every child played at least half the game. He knew his child was going to get to come in and out of the game as much as anybody else, and he wanted to see just how this was going to work.

Before the ball game began, all of the players gathered at half court. They got down on one knee, and the referee explained to them how they were going to call all fouls and all of the violations. Then the referee led in prayer. That was probably the first time this particular dad had seen a referee praying with the teams.

During the first half, his son had gone in and out of the game several times. He was getting equal playing time, which was one of the things the dad expected. But there were a few violations this man felt the referee missed on the court. Still because this dad noticed that this was a different kind of league with a different kind of purpose, he tried to be a good dad and not lose his cool. But as the half came to an end, the score was very close, and this dad was getting a little hot under the collar!

Just about the time he was ready to cut loose and yell at the referee, it was half time. All of the kids left the court and went to the locker rooms where the coaches gave half-time instruction. On the court, an individual came out and shared a devotional thought and a story that had made an impact on his life in the last several weeks. He gave testimony of what God had been doing in his life.

The dad started thinking about what the person on the court was talking about, and the words reminded him that this was just a game (temporary), that there were more important things in life: salvation, character, and self-esteem (eternal). The speaker then led in a word of prayer, and the players came charging back out for the second half.

The game started back up. Once again the man felt like the referee missed a few calls here and there. And, once again, he was getting a little frustrated. His son's team was getting beat pretty badly.

Near the end of the game, his son was dribbling the basketball downcourt. As the boy dribbled toward the basket, the ball bounced off his foot and went out-of-bounds. The referee didn't see it. He thought the ball went off the opponent's foot, so he blew the whistle and said, "White ball." He handed the ball to the man's son.

The little boy looked at the referee and said, "No, Mr. Referee, it's not my ball. It's the other team's ball because it bounced off of *my* foot."

The ref said, "Thank you so much for being honest about that. I appreciate it. Blue ball, we are going back this way."

Well, that just got all over the dad. His son's team was losing. His son had had the chance to get the ball and go down the court and score to try to get them back in the ball game, but, instead, he turned the ball over.

The man just about blew a gasket. Well, it didn't take too much longer for the game to be over, and the man decided to go down there and give the referee a piece of his mind. He wanted to take the ref off to the side and tell him that he was the worst referee he had ever seen in his life.

Once the players had left the court, the dad worked his way through the crowd down to the court. The players were in the locker room with their coaches. The man reached the playing floor and waited for everybody to leave so he could have some one-on-one time with the referee. The gym was just about empty when he came face-to-face with the referee. As he was about to tell him what he thought about his refereeing abilities, his child burst through the door.

"Dad! I got the white star! The most Christlike star! Isn't that great, Dad!"

Even though his son had lost by nearly twenty points, his only comment was, "I got the white star!"

The dad was overwhelmed by his son's reaction. The value of that particular ball game had diminished to nothing, but the impact the coach had on that child made him feel like a winner. The father looked at the referee and said, "For the first time in my life, I don't care what that scoreboard says." He put his arm around his son and walked out the door.

I'm not sure whether that child was a winner because he *learned* something or because he *taught* something, but he was definitely a winner!

Just because a child's team loses the game, doesn't mean he can't win the best sportsmanship star by being a good sport. The team might lose the game, but the best defensive player may have kept the other team from running up the score.

In Upward Basketball, the purpose of giving stars is to focus on the things the kids did right. We encourage them to focus on the positive, not the negative; strengths, not weaknesses. Even in a business or a church, a good leader hires people who have strengths to balance out others' weaknesses.

It is important for parents to be involved as their children experiment with extracurricular activities—sports, music, art, and so forth. Help them see where their strengths and weaknesses lie. Most importantly, help them realize that losing a game or not being the best doesn't make them losers. Losing is something all of us will have come our way. What matters is that we always *learn something*. That's what makes us *winners!*

CHAPTER 8
Children Are Like Clay

Ephesians 2:10 says, "For we are God's workmanship, created in Christ Jesus to do good works, which God prepared in advance for us to do."

When I was first engaged to Leslie, we thought we had all of life's problems figured out. We had dated for nearly two years and had never had an argument—not one. I'm sure a lot of people reading this book are thinking, *Yeah, sure.* But we really didn't—not one argument. I thought, *Man, this is definitely the person I want to marry. No arguing here. Everything's going my way.* That was my first mistake.

Once we were engaged, things started getting intense as we started moving toward our wedding day. One thing led to another and we actually had that long-awaited disagreement. In fact, it led us to cancel our wedding. When that happened, I was devastated. I couldn't imagine that all of those wonderful times we had spent together could be thrown away for no apparent reason.

One night at about midnight, Leslie's father called me. He said, "I'd like to meet you for cheesecake at Denny's."

I have always had a lot of respect for Leslie's dad so I drove over to meet him. He asked me how things were going with Leslie and me. Of course he knew that we were not on good terms. I said, "What are things like at your house?"

He said, "Well, your name has not been mentioned in a sentence with anything good in the last little while. It has been kind of rough." He went on, "I am hearing a lot of negative things about you right now, and before I form an opinion about what I think happened, I want you to tell me your side of the story."

You'll never know how much I appreciated that. I started to tell him my perspective on the matter, and he got a whole lot more information about both sides of the story. The bottom line was that Leslie and I both had some areas that we needed to work on.

I said, "As much as I want it to, I just don't think it's going to work out."

Leslie's father said, "Caz, when you came to me and asked me if you could marry my daughter, do you remember what happened?"

I said, "Yes sir, I do. I asked you if I could have your daughter's hand and all the rest of her in marriage. I told you I would take very good care of her and that I loved her and wanted to make her my wife."

"Do you remember what I said?" he asked.

"Yes, I do. You said, 'I'm going to have to pray about it with my wife and get back to you because she is as much her daughter as she is mine.'" He then made me wait nearly twenty-four hours.

After he and his wife prayed about it together, they came to the conclusion that I was the man. They gave us their blessing.

He now said, "Caz, we didn't just flippantly say yes. We said yes because God told us you were the man for our daughter. Now you and Leslie can decide you are not going to get married for however long you want to, but I know that God told us you are the man."

I said, "I just don't see how that is going to happen based on what we are going through."

Then Leslie's dad told me this story. "Caz, when you were born, you were just a blob of clay on a table, as was Leslie. God began to mold the two of you even while you were in your mothers' wombs. He began to make you look like exactly who you are. And when you were born, God continued to work with you and make you exactly the way He wanted you to be.

"Every situation that comes into your life affects your salvation. Different things affect your character. Different things affect your self-esteem and eventually the kind of person that you are.

"Two years ago, God took you and Leslie—His two pieces of clay—and began making them one, molding them together. He made them just the way He wanted them to be—completely seamless. God has continued to apply paint of different 'colors'—situations and circumstances (many that were out of your control)—that have affected your relationship and made you closer to each other and closer to God.

"Right now to look at that incredible piece of work, it is a very fragile, dry, chalky-looking piece of work—*until* you put it in the fire. When you put it in the fire, in the 'kiln,' things get really hot and all of the impurities start coming to the top. The reason it is in the fire is to burn off those impurities. Before it was put in the fire, it was so fragile that if you dropped it to the ground, it would shatter into a thousand pieces. But when it comes out of the other side of that fire and finally cools down, all of the impurities are gone, and what you've got is an incredibly gorgeous, stunning, vibrant piece of work that God has put together. And what God has put together, no man can take apart. Is that to say that it won't get bumped and bruised and chipped occasionally? No, because it will. And every time it does, there will be a little scar left as a reminder of what happened. But it will never shatter because it is a piece of work that God has put together."

He said, "Today you are in the fire, and those impurities are coming to the top. When they are gone, however, you will be much stronger."

After our talk it didn't take much longer for all of those impurities to get burned off. When Leslie and I cooled down and came back together, we looked at each other and realized just how much we loved each other. When Leslie walked down the aisle at our wedding, we knew there was nothing that could come in our marriage as difficult as what we had been through in that situation. When tough times come, we know the fire will cool, and we will be stronger as a result.

Now that I have children, I marvel at these incredible "pieces of clay" that God has given us and all of the different things that happen in their lives and the opportunities they have that start forming who they are. One wants to be a basketball player; another wants to be a soccer player. The other one simply likes to ride her bike and help her mom fix meals for people. Because she doesn't like to play sports, does that make her a loser? No! She is a winner because she touches lives.

Is that to mean that there are not times the heat gets turned up? Absolutely not. Sometimes it gets hot, and my children are in the fire. At those times we constantly remind them that impurities are coming to the surface, and those impurities are going to be burned off. When they come out on the other side, they will be beautiful pieces of work that God has put together. They are going to learn from those situations. Children need to understand that hard times are going to come in life. It is just a matter of molding and making us into what God wants us to be.

When you are in the fire with your child, will you help build their self-esteem and character or tear it down? Bring out the winner. He *is* in there.

CHAPTER 9

Children Want to Play . . . and Make Lots of Noise!

Children are born with an incredible desire to play.

Suppose we gathered up a group of twenty couples and asked them to bring their children with them. If the children were old enough to take care of themselves, we could say, "Look. The adults are going to have a very important meeting here, and we don't need anybody to bother us. We want you to go outside until we call you." In no time at all, those children would be playing games that we never even heard of. They would simply make up games to play.

Some of the greatest memories I have are of playing with three other friends of mine in our apartment complex using a little baseball bat and a tennis ball. We made the game up. We played on three bases instead of four, and we knocked the balls off of the roofs of the apartments. It was amazing. I had more fun doing that than anything else. I simply had a child's desire to play.

One of the problems that we have right now is that children need to have the freedom to use their own imaginations. In the September 10, 1990, issue of *USA Today,* an article stated, "7 out of 10 kids wished that when they played organized sports, nobody kept score."

That is because they just want to play. P-L-A-Y. The article also said that "4 out of 10 kids wished their parents wouldn't come" to their ball games. That's scary to me. The reason they don't want them to come is because the kids just want to P-L-A-Y. Parents put too much pressure on them to do more than play. Sometimes parents think that excelling is what you must do to have fun. But if children are having fun, they are doing great. If children are having fun, they *will* excel as winners in time.

CHAPTER 10
Treat Children Fairly— but Not Alike

Your children need to know that they are going to be treated fairly in all situations. Many times this can be done creatively.

For example, suppose Mom has just baked a batch of chocolate chip cookies for the neighbors. She made one small plate for the family, and there is only one cookie left on the family plate. Hal and Jill both want that last cookie. How can Mom solve that problem quickly and fairly?

Dr. Kirk Neely, one of the men I was privileged to serve on church staff with, makes this suggestion: "Tell Hal to divide the cookie in half. Then let Jill pick which half she would like to eat. You can be sure that Hal will divide that cookie as perfectly down the middle as he can!"

Treating children fairly, however, does not mean treating them alike in all situations. Every child's situation is different at different ages.

For example, when we go to the swimming pool in the summer, Lauren and Keighlee are old enough to stay without an adult. Leslie and all the girls go and stay for half a day. Then, when Mama is ready to go home, she takes our youngest, Mari Caroline, home with her.

All the way home, Mari Caroline complains, "It's not fair, it's not fair. Why don't I get to stay?"

"Well, honey," Leslie says, "it's just one of those things. You are not old enough to take care of yourself yet."

Three hours later, the big girls roll in. As they walk in the door, they see Mari Caroline playing in the playroom.

Soon after arriving home, their mother says, "Lauren, Keighlee, I need you to get the clothes out of the dryer, fold them, and put them away."

The two suddenly protest: "Wait a minute, that's not fair. Mari Caroline is sitting there playing. Why didn't she do this while we were gone?" (What a good time to light the fire in the kiln!)

My wife responds with a truism that I have used many times since: "Along with privileges come responsibilities."

How incredible is that? The privilege of staying at the pool brings more responsibilities. Because they are older, they have more responsibilities. The more freedom they have, the more responsibility they have. If they have the freedom to stay at the pool, they also have the responsibility to pull more weight at the house.

It is also important to note that as Mari Caroline gets more freedom to do other things, she also will get more responsibility. With privileges come responsibilities: an important lesson to learn—at any age!

CHAPTER 11

Children Are
the Good Soil

Your child is the good soil, and you are the seed caster. The passage of Scripture about the sower and the seed is a familiar one. It is the first parable that Jesus ever told.

In Mark 4:1–20 Jesus told this story of a farmer who began spreading seed. The seed fell over four different kinds of soil. Some of it fell on good soil; some fell on thorny soil; some fell on rocky soil; and some of it fell on the hard path. The seed on the good soil took root, grew, and formed branches and leaves, eventually producing fruit that multiplied thirty, sixty, and a hundred times.

Then Jesus said that some of the seed fell *among* the thorns. In other words, the thorns were already there. When the seeds fell among the thorns, they sprouted just like those on the good soil. But after those seeds had branches and leaves, the thorns that were growing at the same time squeezed out |

and choked the plant before it could ever produce fruit. The plant looked the same, but it could not produce.

Some of the seed fell along the rocky path and sprouted up quickly. When the sun came out, however, and the day heated up, because the root was shallow, the plant withered.

And then there was the seed that fell along the hard path. That's the seed that the birds came by and ate; they snatched it up, and it was gone. It never took root to begin with.

I have heard many sermons on this passage of Scripture. Of course, the soils represent the hearts of all the people in the world, and the seed represents the good news—the gospel, the love of Jesus Christ.

One day I was preparing to do a message on this Scripture even though I didn't know why the Lord wanted me to share this message at that church I was invited to. I just couldn't figure it out. I felt like everybody had heard it, and I just didn't want to do something that everyone had already heard.

I prayed, "Lord, You speak to me in what You want to say to me, and if anybody else can learn from it, that will be great." As I studied that passage, I realized a couple of things.

Jesus actually was the one who interpreted that parable a few paragraphs later. He told His disciples that the seed that was thrown among the good soil represents people who ask Jesus into their lives. When those people grow, they are going to produce fruit—they are going to tell other people about the good news of Jesus Christ. Those people will tell more people, and the numbers will continue to multiply—thirty-, sixty-, and a hundredfold.

The seed thrown among the thorns was the one I probably learned the most about when I was reading. The word *among* jumped out at me. That word means that the thorns were already there, just as the rocks and the hard path were already there.

In verses 18–19 Jesus said the thorns that were already there represent three things. They represent:

- "the worries of this life,"
- "the deceitfulness of wealth," and
- "the desire for other things."

In thinking about these three things, I considered my own children. When my daughter was three, did she have any idea what the worries of this world were? She had no clue. The deceitfulness of wealth? The desire for other things? None of these things crossed her mind.

I realized that the thorns described in the Bible represent things that are learned. The longer we live, the more television, radio, newspaper, and even people influence us. We learn it all, the good and the bad.

So if "thorns" are things that are learned, then the good soil must be the younger children. The older we get, the more the thorns come in and turn into rocks, and eventually the rocks turn into a hard path. I think Jesus was trying to tell us to share Christ with children at an early age. They are the good soil!

Unfortunately, very few people are out there casting the seed before the good soil becomes thorny and rocky and hard. It is our responsibility to share the love of Jesus Christ with the good soil. One of my greatest burdens is to raise the number of those casting seed on the good soil and lower the number casting on the hardened path. As long as you understand the moldability of a child, you will understand the importance of those younger years when you are with them.

There is one more important point here. Remember the seed in this parable is the gospel of Jesus Christ. You can have all kinds of places to plant the seed, but until somebody actually *takes* the seed and throws it out on the ground, *nothing is going to happen.*

I don't think it is a mistake that Jesus used the example of fruit in His illustration. If you cut open an apple and look inside, what do you see? Seeds. If you cut open an orange and look inside, what do you see? Seeds. If you cut open a watermelon, what do you see? Seeds.

Jesus refers to those who have come to know the Lord as fruit. I am the fruit of somebody else's tree, so what is in me? Seeds. I have seeds that need to be cast to others. My desire is to create "seed casters." We need people to open up themselves and spread the seeds that are within them all around.

You can be the greatest-looking apple around. You can be the apple of your Father's eye, but if you set that apple on a counter, even though the apple looks great, you will never have another apple unless you take the seeds in that apple and cast them out on the ground. Then and only then will it produce other fruit.

As parents, coaches, teachers, or whatever our role with children, we are the ones who are the seed casters. We are the ones who have to take the seeds of the gospel and cast them—especially among the children. The longer we wait to throw seeds out there, the more opportunity for "thorns" to come into our children's lives. It doesn't matter how hard we try to keep them out; we can home school, turn off our televisions, never buy magazines or newspapers, or whatever the case may be, but the older our children get, the more thorns are going to come into their lives.

CHAPTER 12

Circle of Criticism
Vs. Circle of Praise

Another growing challenge to instill in your child at a young age is the respect for authority. One of the things in Upward Basketball that affects the relationship between a referee, a coach, a parent, and a child is what we call the "circle of criticism."

When the referee makes a call in a ball game, it's entirely up to the coach how the rest of the ball game is going to go. If the coach begins to criticize and make negative comments, then that in turn gives "permission" to the parent to do the same thing. When a child sees a parent yelling at a referee, who is a form of authority, the child gets the message that it is OK. Although the child may not yell at the referee in that game or even that year, the idea is planted in his brain that it is OK to yell at a form of authority. The referee is doing his job as an authority figure even if he has made a mistake. The coach's response influences the response of the parent, which influences the response of the players.

The alternative we try to teach in Upward Basketball is the "circle of praise" as opposed to the "circle of criticism." In the circle of praise, when the authority figure makes a call, the coach encourages, lifts up, and respects that decision. As a result, the parents usually do the same thing. The children see what the parents are doing, and all of a sudden, the circle of praise actually encourages the referee to be the very best he can be.

I think these circles can be applied in our families as well. The circle of criticism often begins with previous generations. If grandparents were critical and demeaning as opposed to being loving adults placed in a position of authority, that's the way they treated our parents as children. As a result, our parents may have treated us in a similar way. When we are children we often think, *I will never be like my mother or father.* Yet, as we get older, we catch ourselves saying, "I am turning into my dad." We may joke about it, but if the action we are perpetuating is a bad one, we need to make a change—the circle of criticism needs to be transformed into a circle of praise.

Whether we like it or not, if we don't do something about it, our children are going to turn into the people that we are, the people that our parents were. Just understanding that process means that we *can* break the chain. We have the ability to change that circle of criticism into a circle of praise. Of course, if we came from a good circle, we have the opportunity to keep that circle going.

The exciting thing is that it is not unchangeable. As far as a parent is concerned in the circle of praise, when you start encouraging your child and lifting that child up, that's the encouragement he is going to pass on to his children because he is an outpouring of who you are. It's an easy thing to change circles just by realizing who you are and where you are as a person.

While growing up, I sometimes made excuses when I didn't get one of my chores done. For example, often before Dad went to work, he said, "Now, son, I want you to mow the yard, trim the bushes, weed-eat, and blow off the driveway."

When he'd come home from work and it wasn't done yet, he'd say, "Well, son, why didn't you mow the yard?"

"Well, I was going to but—"

Dad stopped me before I even finished my sentence. "Let me just stop you right there, son."

"But, Dad, I had all of these things I had to do . . . ."

"Son, anytime you have a sentence separated by the word *but*, you can forget anything before the *but* and start listening to everything after that word. That's the real story."

"Well, I was going to mow the yard, and I was going to do it this morning; I was even going to trim the hedges today, but . . . ." The truth was, something else became more important to me. I had a deeper burden for something else inside of me—like going to the movies or playing basketball with my friends—and that became more important. In other words, respecting my father's authority was not top priority. That was a bad choice!

Jesus, however, showed us how to make the right choices when we respond to authority. Jesus was God and He was man, so He had the same temptations we do—but His responses were always perfect.

When Jesus went to Gethsemane just before He was crucified, it had to be His darkest hour. In Matthew 26:39–44, the Bible tells us that Jesus prayed and talked to His Father, saying, "Father, if there is any way You can take this cup from Me, I really don't want to go through this, *but* [here comes what is really important] not My will, but Yours be done" (paraphrased).

You see, Jesus reversed what we normally do. He talked about all of the things that He felt, then said, ". . . *but* I don't want to do what I want to do; I want to do what *You* want Me to do."

Even when He prayed a second time, He said, "Father, if there is any way You can take this away from Me, I wish You would do that, *but* not My will, but Yours be done." Even a third time he did the same thing: "Not My will, *but* Yours be done."

Parents are often tempted to "parent" selfishly. We want to spend more time with our children, and we don't mean to embarrass them at their ball games by yelling at the referee, *but* . . . we become more concerned about something that is important to us. Many times we try to make excuses for what we do, and look at the mistakes we make! An engram for Jesus was to do God's will. That's simply the way He thought 100 percent of the time—*not My will, but Yours be done.* Shouldn't it be the same for us as we strive to follow Christ's example?

CHAPTER 13

Immediate Discipline

Billy Graham has said that all children should be involved in sports at one time in their lives because it is one of the last things out there that has immediate discipline for doing something wrong.

For example, if you double dribble, the ball will be taken away from you and given to the other team. If you hit somebody on the hand while trying to play defense, you are going to get a foul. There's a penalty for wrongdoing in sports— "immediate discipline." (One of the biggest mistakes made in children's sports today is not calling all violations on young players learning the game. If you don't call it all, you are only confusing the child and setting him up to be angry when you do call the violation later.)

In today's world there is very little immediate discipline, even in our schools. When someone does something wrong, he or she gets sent to the 55 principal, who calls Mom or Dad, and then everyone talks about the "problem" for a few weeks. There is no immediate discipline. I think this sends a confusing message to our children.

In sports, however, if children realize there is immediate discipline for wrongdoing, it will make an impact on them that will deter them from repeating the same thing again.

When I was in third grade, my brother and sister bought me a basketball for Christmas. I had never played sports before I was in the third grade, but I used to love watching my brother play. He was an incredible athlete, and I always wanted to play ball like my brother. Once I got my basketball, the first thing I wanted to do was go outside and shoot; I wanted to play a game.

My brother asked, "Do you really want to be a good player someday?"

"I really do," was my reply.

He said, "If you really want to be a good player, there are a few things that you have to learn before you can ever play the game."

I said, "All right. What's that?"

He said, "All I want you to do for awhile is practice dribbling. Go outside and dribble with your right hand for an hour and then dribble with your left for an hour. I want you to take all of one day and just dribble with your right hand, then take all of the next day and dribble with your left hand. Back and forth. When you get to the point where you can dribble with either hand the same way, then you will be ready to go to the next step."

For a couple of weeks I dribbled to school with my right hand and dribbled back with my left hand. I dribbled around the block with one hand and back around the block with the other hand. I loved to play with that ball. I couldn't wait to play a real game.

One day (before I was really ready) a coach from our little elementary school team saw me dribbling everywhere I went. He came up to me and asked if I would be interested in playing for the elementary school team. Most of those kids were older than me, so it was a big deal for me to be invited to go out there and play. When I showed up on that basketball court, it was the first time in my life that I had ever been on an actual court. All I had was a basketball and the ability to dribble with my right hand and my left. That's all I knew.

We were having a practice scrimmage game among our own team, but we had a referee. My team had on blue shirts, and the other team had on white shirts. I'll never forget when another kid threw me the basketball and the exhilaration I felt wanting to dribble down the court and score a basket.

I dribbled the ball about three times and this guy in a white shirt jumps up in front of me and yells, "Heeeey!" It scared me to death! I just stopped, grabbed the ball, and tucked it underneath my arm. He backed off a little bit, so I thought, *Well, that's better.* I started dribbling again toward my basket. The referee started blowing his whistle and chasing me, yelling, "You can't do that!" He grabbed the ball away from me and gave it to the other team. I thought, *Man, what in the world was that all about?*

After the other team came down and scored, someone threw the basketball to me again. I dribbled about three times, and the same guy in a white shirt jumped in front of me again and yelled, "Heeeey!" It scared me to death again! I thought, *What's he doing?* Once again, I tucked the ball under my arm.

Just as I was about to start dribbling, I remembered the referee saying not to dribble (at least that's what I thought he meant). So I just tucked the ball under my arm and started running toward the basket.

The referee blew his whistle and yelled, "You can't do that!" He chased after me, took the ball away, and gave it to the other team.

Well, I wasn't in that game three minutes before I hated it. It was the worst experience in my life. I mean, I had been so excited about playing basketball, but the two times I got to touch the ball, the referee took it away from me. I was a basket case. I went home and cried. It was terrible!

When my brother came home, he asked, "What's the matter?" I told him everything that had happened.

He said, "Well, all you have to do is play by the rules."

So I said, "What rules?"

He told me all about double dribbling, traveling, out-of-bounds, three seconds, reaching in, and all kinds of rules. I had seen my brother play, but I had never really paid any attention to what the referee had been doing.

I said, "Well, if I had just known these things, I could have done better. I could have played by the rules."

He said, "That's exactly right. Just go by the rules!"

The next time I went out on the court, I played by the rules, and basketball soon became my favorite game.

When I think about children being winners in life, a lot of the reason they don't know how to become winners is because they *don't know the rules*. If they understand the rules, they are going to win in the game of life.

Unfortunately, parents often take discipline way too lightly when children are young. We don't "blow the whistle" as often as we should when "refereeing" our children as they learn the rules. We don't provide immediate discipline. Then when they are older, we wonder why they don't obey. Well . . . when the opportunity arises, it is too late to prepare.

The things we do as parents instill in our children the rules of life. As long as they understand the rules, they will enjoy life.

And in learning by immediate discipline for wrongdoing, our children will enjoy the game a whole lot more.

As Dr. James Dobson says, you can't be a good parent from your easy chair. If your small child is walking toward the hot stove, are you going to remain in your recliner and say, "Don't touch that. Don't touch that. That's going to burn you! Don't touch that"? Or are you going to run over and stop him? You may even spank his hand to show that he doesn't need to touch it. Perhaps a little spank on the hand will save him the pain he would have felt from the burn on his hand. It's a discipline that you want to be sure the child learns so that something more detrimental doesn't happen.

A friend of mine told me the story of his neighbor's three-year-old child who walked out the back door, fell into the swimming pool, and drowned. What would you do to prevent that from happening to your child? I think you would answer, "Whatever it takes!" You would hold him back; you would lock the door in your house. Even if he cried for an hour and a half because he couldn't go out there, even if you had to spank him in love, you would still make sure he was safe. You would be saving the child's life by teaching him not to go near the pool without an adult. By forcing him to do what is right, you teach a life lesson. That child doesn't know what he doesn't know, and that's a teachable moment. Children must develop a respect for authority, and the best way for them to learn that is through immediate discipline of some kind.

What's more, as children learn rules through the use of immediate discipline, they develop a conscience. Then when they are faced with a decision between right and wrong, the "referee" deep within "blows the whistle" to let them know, "You can't do that." That is also what the Holy Spirit does for us as Christians. Every time we make a bad choice, our "heart whistle" blows, letting us know we are on the wrong track.

My prayer is that as my children get older, they will know the rules and listen to what God is saying through their consciences. That way they will develop the self-discipline they need to be successful, godly adults.

Immediate discipline, respect for authority, being prepared in advance before the opportunities arise: all of these things weave together to bring out the winner in a child!

CHAPTER 14

Children Need Flexibility

Flexibility can often open the door for a teachable moment with your child.

One of the things we teach children in Upward Basketball is to memorize a Bible verse each week. I was refereeing an Upward Basketball game one time when a second-grade girls' team was playing. There were only about thirty-five seconds left on the clock. Everybody was trying to get the girls to score a basket before the clock ran out. Well, the ball went out-of-bounds. I ran over, got it, and handed it to a little girl. I said, "Hurry, honey. Throw the ball in. You only have a few seconds to get up there and shoot before the game is over."

But she said, "Before I do, can I tell you my memory verse?"

I thought, *We've got thirty-five seconds. It's game time. We've got to go! The clock's running.*

"I want to tell you my memory verse," she said. | **61**

I dropped to one knee, put the ball down, and said, "Tell me. What is that memory verse?"

She quoted her Bible verse, smiled, and said, "There, I did it."

I said, "Wow, you sure did."

Of course the clock ran out, and everyone looked at me from the stands like I was crazy. Still, that child taught me a lesson that day. It was incredible. We need the flexibility to be able to listen to a child and take the time you need to hear what he or she has to say. In the past I might have said to myself, "Get her down the court, score the basket, then listen to what she has to say." But that's not what she needed at that moment. She needed me to realize how important that verse was to her. So, is flexibility important?

Bill Hybels says in *Becoming a Contagious Christian* that you have to earn the right to invite. In other words, you have to earn the right to be able to share the important things with your children. If you are going to cast these seeds—whether it be to your children, to your friends, or to your neighbors—you have to earn the right to share the Lord with them. You have to earn the right to make an impact on them by your actions and your relationship with them. This philosophy has had a big impact on me as far as giving advice to my own children.

My wife is especially good at listening. She encourages our girls with open ears, heart, and mind. Our children come in and tell us stories that, quite frankly, might cause other moms and dads to fall out onto the floor. However, my wife has taught me that if you drop your jaw and freak out when children say these things to you, the continuation of these stories will come to a screeching halt—especially if your first reaction is, "You need to stop hanging around them. You need to find new friends."

Leslie has earned the right to share her opinion by listening to the girls and waiting for them to be open to her advice before she gives it. She simply loves them for who they are, and they know it! An enormous number of children come to our house to spend the night with our girls. In most cases when they get there, they pull up a chair and begin talking with Leslie and asking her, "What do I do about this? What do I do about that?" She has an opportunity to minister to those girls because she earned the right to be able to share with them. Leslie is very honest with them and truly cares for them. They respect that.

During every level of our children's development, they ask about things, not because they are trying to shock us but because they genuinely want to know. For example, when a first grader comes home and asks you what a cuss word means, your reaction should never be surprise. Ask your child where he or she heard the word. Then explain to him or her what it means and that it is not a word that needs to be repeated. Your child is not the wrongdoer but the victim of what someone else said. Rather than gasping and covering your mouth with your hand, take this opportunity to teach biblical principles about how to respond when a friend uses a bad word.

In the same way, when older children ask questions about morality, sex, or other "touchy" subjects, answer them honestly. If they want to know, they will keep asking until they get the information. Better that you give them correct, Bible-based facts than their peers instruct them on the playground or in the bathroom at school. If they ask, deal with it, whether you think they (or you) are ready or not. Being flexible could be a matter of attitude rather than schedule!

CHAPTER 15
Developing Your Child's Self-Esteem

In building your child's self-esteem, one of the things that your child needs is an equal opportunity for improvement. In Upward Basketball, we make sure that children play against children of equal ability. This creates an equal opportunity for improvement.

I love the game of basketball. I love to play basketball, and I love to get better at basketball. But if I were trying to get better by spending a couple of hours playing one-on-one with Michael Jordan, I wouldn't get any better. Especially if I played "make it, take it." I would only be a rebounder. I wouldn't get any better playing the game. Michael Jordan is a phenomenal player, and he is way out of my league. I would never get any better trying to play somebody that is so far above my ability.

It is important to try to provide an equal playing field for children, especially during a game.

Think about your own desire to get better and better at all you do. If you play against someone of equal or slightly better ability, then you work hard to improve. You do the best you can do and you find yourself in an environment in which you *can* improve. The practice, the stamina, and the striving to stay with your equally talented opponent makes you a better player. That is true of any skill you try to master.

If you are always put in a situation where you can never reach the level of what is expected of you, however, you become tempted to throw in the towel. You may just quit. Sometimes parents place the bar too high for their children too soon. The children see an impossible task instead of an attainable goal, and they never get better.

A huge milestone for me was realizing that God was not nearly as concerned about my ability as He was with my *availability*. I realized that as long as I gave my life to Him and I was willing to do what He wanted me to do and go where He wanted me to go, I was a winner. I often prayed, "If you want to use me, here I am. I'm not claiming myself as being anything special. But I'm available to do whatever You want me to do."

Many times I have questioned my own ability to do certain things. For example, I knew I was called into the ministry, but I was scared to accept that call because I didn't want to go to Africa. Also, I didn't want to be single. Still, I couldn't release the fact that if I was called into the ministry, I had to be available to do whatever God wanted me to do, even if that meant going to Africa or living life as a single person.

I struggled all through my dating life. I was never truly happy dating anybody. I finally said, "OK, Lord, if You want me to be single, I'll be single." And it was almost in that breath that I met my bride-to-be. Once I became obedient to God's call, I found that He didn't really want me to be single. He simply wanted me to be available to be single and obedient to Him *if* that was His plan.

Sometimes the availability is all He wants. Sometimes God calls us to do things that we aren't comfortable with just because He wants us to be available to Him. He says, "OK, you're available and that's great. This activity is not what I want you to do right now, but now I know you are committed to do *whatever* I need you to do." This must be exactly how Abraham felt as he climbed that mountain to sacrifice his son.

Children want to be available. At a very young age children want to be involved in everything we do. Unfortunately, we often push them away or tell them they are not skilled enough or big enough to do what we are doing. If we do this too often, eventually the availability they so freely offer goes away. We must encourage their availability by giving them tasks they have the ability to do, being careful to not give them things that are over and above their abilities.

Children need an equal opportunity to serve. God doesn't care about their abilities; He cares about their availability. Our children are never going to get to the point where they want to serve if they don't realize they are winners first. If they don't know they are learning or teaching something in the game plan of life, they'll never serve in any way because they won't think they have anything to offer.

Some of the greatest advice I ever received was: "Never turn down a gift from a child—not even a half-eaten cookie with slime on it"—because it teaches the joy of giving to that child. I would add to that advice: "Never, never turn down the help of a child." It will teach the joy of serving and availability!

CHAPTER 16

Physical Fitness Affects Self-Esteem

To be a winner, your child needs to develop healthy habits. This is a pretty important fact as far as practical things for your children are concerned. If a child has a choice between eating green beans or a candy bar, it's not going to take them long to figure out which one they like better. But they don't know the health impact of choosing the candy bar over the green beans every single day. They just know the candy bar tastes good. If a child only eats chocolate and fats, he has no idea of the consequences on his health in the years to come. Therefore, parents must provide the willpower for their kids until the children are able to make their own decisions about what to eat.

Children love to play. Unfortunately, parents sometimes discourage healthy exercise. We are scared to let our children go outside by themselves, but it's not always easy for us to go outside and play with them. Therefore we let the television become our baby-sitter. Eventually, this turns them into couch potatoes. We need to put our children into active situations every chance we can.

Mike Murdock once said, "If you want something you have never had, then you have to do something you have never done."

Often, a child's physical appearance doesn't bother him or her at all, especially when he or she is at that phase where "everybody is just like me." When he gets to the next level, however—where he realizes, "Hey, not everybody is just like me"—his attitude changes. Then he says to himself, *Maybe I'm not supposed to be this way. Maybe I'm supposed to be like that.* When that situation arises, it's usually too late to prepare. If your child is overweight and out of shape because he has not exercised, it is usually because of the choices you made for that child when he was young.

Here's a little insight for new parents. Every one of your child's fat cells are formed by the time he or she is between the ages of two and four. When the child gets older, these cells don't multiply; they just increase and decrease in size. This means that the fewer fat cells he or she has, the less likely he or she is to increase in size and the easier it will be to maintain normal weight. (Still, she will need to control her size by proper exercise and a healthy diet.) Young children, however, have no idea what the facts are on fat cells. Therefore, it is up to parents to teach children good health habits from the beginning.

Children need positive affirmation. Parents have the greatest opportunity to build a child's self-esteem and help him realize he *is* a winner. Proper health and a mobile body are major parts of a child's self-esteem.

CHAPTER 17

Do It Right—
the First Time

Your children need structure. As mentioned before, your children are going to be a natural reflection of who you are. This may be a little frightening when you see them doing something, and you think, *I can't believe they are doing that.*

Yet when you get to your office, you may catch yourself doing something similar. You realize, *That child's doing what I do. I wonder why that is!*

I attended a time management seminar to learn ways to better organize my days. One of the things the seminar leader asked us to do was write down three things we had accomplished over the last twelve months that we were very excited about.

He gave some personal examples. "(1) For the first time in my life, I was able to do one hundred sit-ups. (2) My company was able to go over the new benchmark that we had put out there in front of ourselves, and we reached all of our goals financially. (3) I celebrated my twenty-fifth wedding anniversary."

Following his instructions, we each wrote down three things we were excited about accomplishing that year.

Then he said, "OK. The next thing I want you to do is a little tougher. I want you to write down three things you are disappointed about this last year. These are things that you really wanted to accomplish but didn't." He mentioned a few of his own disappointments: "(1) I wanted to work less each week—not put in sixty or seventy hours—but sometimes I still did. (2) I wanted to start a savings account but I didn't do it." And then he said something that broke my heart. He said, "(3) I want to tell you one of my greatest disappointments. I coached my son's baseball team (he is ten years old), and my biggest disappointment this year was that he didn't win any ball games."

Man, I almost jumped up on my chair and yelled, "You missed it!" He said that his greatest disappointment was that *his child* didn't win a single ball game. That man, a leader and a father, placed *his* accomplishment and disappointment on what *his son* did on the ball field. That is an enormous amount of pressure to put on any child. That father needed to turn around and ask himself, "What did I learn from not winning any ball games? What did my child learn from this season? What life lessons can we both learn here?" His child was no less a winner because he didn't win a ball game. But considering the father's attitude, I wonder if his child realized he is a winner.

Those are the kinds of things that we are trying to avoid in raising our children.

Now, back to the seminar. The next thing the leader said was really very challenging. He asked, "What do you think was the cause of your disappointment?"

That was easy for me. Many of my disappointments are the result of procrastinating and settling for second-best, putting things off until the last minute. I am disappointed in myself when I have to cram to get things done. One of our guiding principles at my office is to do everything first-class—organized and detailed. The only way to do that is if I plan things out ahead of time. The reason I don't do everything that I want to do at my office, or even at home, is that I have not planned ahead in every situation. And when I don't do everything first-class—organized and detailed—I settle for second-best. Therefore, the thing that caused my disappointment was procrastination.

For example, when I walk in the house and take my shoes off, I throw them on the floor. Why? Because I procrastinate putting them in my closet. Why do I procrastinate? Because it takes too long to go upstairs, put them in my closet, and come all the way back downstairs.

When I ask my children to make their beds, their first thought is, *It takes too long,* so they wait until the last minute before they go to school and then they pull up the cover, throw the pillow on the bed, and come running down the steps.

When I ask, "Why didn't you make your bed? You just threw the covers up," they say, "Well, it takes too long."

In other words, my kids are doing the same things they see me do. They procrastinate because they see me procrastinate. In the end they settle for less because they have to do the job at the last second instead of planning ahead to do it.

Now we have a little "McCaslin Proverb" that we put on the refrigerator of our home that says: "It is faster to do something right the first time than it is to do it twice."

My daily "to do list" is now a "things to do right the first time" list. When I'm working through my list, I still look at some of the things I have to do and say, "Ah! It is going to take too long!" Nonetheless, I simply decide I'm going to do it right the first time. As much as I hate it, I'm going to do it right the first time and get it completely done the right way. Then when I am done with it, I can move on.

I'm working on creating a new engram for myself and in my children. The new engram is to do it right the first time. If I can help my children learn that one philosophy, it will follow them for the rest of their lives, impacting them forever. They will ultimately be able to accomplish more in life because it is much faster to do it right the first time than it is to do it twice. It is an engram that will pull out the winner in each of them.

CHAPTER 18
Creating Trustworthiness

We are creating trustworthiness in our children every day. As they get older we need to give them more responsibility. If we realize this earlier as parents, then what we are doing is creating children who can be trusted. This has everything to do with doing things right the first time. Every time our children do something right the first time, we need to acknowledge that and praise them for not procrastinating.

One big key to creating trustworthiness in a child is problem prevention. A lot of people feel the best way to teach a child something is to let him make a mistake and suffer the consequences; then he will never do it again. Sometimes that happens by accident, whether you want to do it that way or not. We talked about a young child walking into a kitchen and putting her hands on a stove. If you caught her before she put her hands on the stove, you could discipline her and save her from pain. If you don't catch her, however, and she puts her hand on the stove, the lesson is much more severe. She still learned a lesson and will never put her hand on the stove again. But that's not the way you would have chosen for her to learn it. You don't want your child to have to go through suffering to learn everything.

As our children grow up, learning from mistakes—figuring out things for themselves—becomes more dangerous. You don't want your child to figure out for himself that it's not a good idea for him to drink and drive. You don't want him to figure out for himself it's not a good idea to do drugs. In many cases, it's going to be too late; he or she might not get a second chance. How do you prevent those things from happening?

My "Twelveteen" Lesson in Trustworthiness

I want to tell you my favorite lesson my father ever taught me. It happened when I was about "twelveteen" (you know, that's when you can't wait to be a teenager. You think you are old enough to do everything that teenagers can do, but you can't. You can't quite drive, but you don't need a baby-sitter. You are at that terrible age of in between.) My "twelveteen" birthday was in April, right toward the end of the school year. I lived in Atlanta, and a lot of my friends were getting passes to Six Flags amusement park. It opened up only on the weekend in the early spring but every day all summer. The passes were pretty expensive, but if you bought one, you could go as many times as you liked for a full year. All of my buddies were getting passes, and they were going every weekend. I said, "Dad, I really *need* a Six Flags pass."

He kept saying, "Well, we'll think about it," but that's all that happened.

Finally, my birthday rolled around. When I woke up that morning and walked in the kitchen, there on the table was a card—nothing else. No presents, nothing. I opened the card, and sure enough, there was just enough money to buy a Six Flags season pass. On the card my Dad had written, "Son, I hope you have a great time at Six Flags. I will take you anytime you want to go, pick you up anytime you need to be picked up. This pass only comes with one rule: Never on Sunday. I love you, Dad."

I said, "Man, I can handle that. After six days at Six Flags, I'll take a break. Everybody needs a day off."

However, it was still springtime, and Six Flags wasn't even open during the week yet because we were still in school. Every weekend I would call one of my buddies. "Hey, Bob. You want to go to Six Flags? We are going on Saturday; my dad's driving and picking up."

"No, man, I've already been four times. I'm kind of tired of it." OK.

Next friend. "Hey, Jim. We are going to Six Flags. My dad is driving and picking up; you want to go on Saturday?"

"No, man. I've been going with Bob. I am kind of tired of it."

Nobody I called about going to Six Flags wanted to go. And I had this Six Flags pass burning a hole in my pocket. I wanted to go so bad it wasn't even funny.

One day my next-door neighbor, Skip, called me and said, "Caz, we are going to Six Flags; do you want to go?"

I said, "Yeah, man! I can't wait! You just tell me when. Do you want my dad to drive? Do you want him to pick up? He can do either one."

He said, "No, my whole family is going. We are going to ride out with them, and they told me that once we get there, we could do our own thing. And they can bring us home too."

"Great. When are we going?"

"Sunday."

I said, "Man, you got to be kidding me. Why aren't we going on Saturday?"

"Well, my dad has to work on Saturday, so we are going to go on Sunday."

I said, "No way; we have to go on Saturday."

He said, "I can't go on Saturday because I am going on Sunday. Just ask your dad. What's the matter with asking?"

I thought, *Yeah, what's wrong with asking?* So I walked into the den. There sat Dad in his big recliner. He had his newspaper. It seemed like I could always find my dad in that chair, reading the paper! I walked in there and said, "Hey, Dad."

"Yep?"

"Skip and his family are going to Six Flags, and they want to know if I can go."

"Sure, son, no problem. When are you going?"

"Sunnndaum," I said with my hand partially covering my mouth.

"What was that?"

"Sunnndaum," I said, again trying to muffle my reply.

"Son, I can't hear you. When are they going?"

"Sunday, Dad! They are going on Sunday!"

He said, "I thought we had a rule about that, son."

I said, "I know, but Dad, this thing has been burning a hole in my pocket for like three weeks, and I have just *got* to go. What do you think, Dad? Can I go? Just this once?"

Well, this is the great thing about parents. They can say yes, or they can say no. Or they can say, "I'm leaving it up to you" (I always hated that one). So my dad pulled the paper down, peered over the top, and said, "I'll tell you what, son. I'm leaving it up to you," and went back to reading his paper. He didn't think twice about it.

So I went back to my room like any red-blooded American "twelveteen"-year-old and called my buddy and said, "I'm in there! I'm in! I'm going! I'm with you! See you Sunday."

Sunday morning rolled around. Mom, Dad, my brothers, and my sister got ready to go to church while I put on my shorts and tennis shoes and a T-shirt. I said, "See y'all later; I'm going to Six Flags!"

I went next door to Skip's. We got in the car and drove off. Just about the time we were pulling into the park, I looked at my watch and it was 9:45. I thought, *Hmmm, Mom and Dad and the family are pulling into the church parking lot by now.*

We walked in the gate. I had my pass and showed it to the guy. "Come on in!"

Yes sir, buddy, we walked right in there. When we got inside the door, Skip's family looked at us and said, "OK, boys, we will see y'all around 9:00 P.M., right here, same place."

There we were, two twelveteen-year-old boys, by ourselves in the Six Flags park, able to do whatever we wanted for the next eleven hours. Yet my conscience was killing me. I was as sick to my stomach as I ever had been. I thought to myself, *What have I done? This is so ridiculous. My dad was kind enough to give me this pass—with only one rule—and here I am blowing it.* And now I had to live with it for the next eleven hours.

It was the worst day of my life. Every time I looked at my watch, I would picture where my family was: "Well, they're in church." "Well, they are at the Kentucky Fried Chicken." "Well, they are home watching baseball."

Later that night, "Well, they are back at church." Then later, "They're watching *Hee-Haw* and eating Mom's Sunday night special—hot dogs and baked beans."

I walked in the door about 9:30, and my dad was sitting in the same ol' chair. He pulled the paper down, and all he said was, "Did you have a good time, son?" Then he went right back to reading the paper.

I said, "No, Dad, I didn't." I went to my room and never said another word about it.

Now, that's not the end of my "twelveteen" lesson. When we are around twelve or thirteen years old, we start getting opportunities to go to parties we probably shouldn't go to. Some parents of kids that age take on the philosophy, "Well, if they are going to try smoking or drinking or some other crazy stuff, I want them to do it at my house." The parents allow parties with too much freedom, including the freedom of the kids being by themselves. The parties are not well monitored, and it doesn't take long for this knowledge to get around to the other parents.

So, school was almost out for the summer. Terry, a guy in my class, called me up and asked me to come to an end-of-the-year party. I knew what kind of party it was and the kind of things that might go on there. My mom and dad also knew what kind of party it could be. (Parents are pretty smart.)

When my friend invited me to this party, he said, "Man, you don't want to miss it. This is going to be the greatest party ever."

I said, "Terry, I don't think I will be able to go."

Terry didn't give up easily. "Well, just ask," he said. "What could that hurt?"

"All right. I'll ask."

So I walked into the den and said, "Hey, Dad."

"Yes, sir?" He pulled his paper down to make eye contact.

"I just wanted to know if I could go to Terry's house for a party this Friday."

Remember, Dad could have said yes. He could have said no. He could have said, "I'm leaving it up to you." He looked me right in the eye and said, "No, son, sorry. You can't go to that one." Then he went right back to his paper.

"Dad!" I protested.

"Sorry, son. Can't do it." End of the story. I stayed home.

Later that summer, Dave, another friend of mine, called. Dave and his family went to Myrtle Beach every year, and every year the children got to bring a friend.

Dave called me up and said, "Caz, we are going to the beach for a week, and we always get to bring a friend. This year you're the man! You get to go with me. It's not going to cost you a thing. We are gonna feed you; we are gonna swim; it's gonna be awesome."

I said, "Yeah, baby! When is it going to be?"

"The week of July 4. That's when we always go," Dave said.

"AAGGHH!"

"What's the matter?"

I groaned, "I think we are going out of town that week—family vacation."

"Well, just ask."

"OK. I'll ask!"

So I went to my dad that night when he got home, and he was reading his paper as usual. I said, "Hey, Dad."

"Yes, sir?"

"You know Dave? He's going to Myrtle Beach. He gets to bring a friend with him, and he wants to know if I can go. It's not going to cost a thing, and I'll be out of your hair for six or seven days. It's gonna be fantastic."

Dad nods. "That sounds pretty good. When are you going?"

I said, "It's the week of the Fourth of July."

He pulled his paper down and said, "Son, you know that is the week that we drive to Pennsylvania with the family to see Nana."

"Yeah, I know," I groaned. "I'm just trying to weigh out the value of the two things here. You know, Myrtle Beach, sun, fun—or Nana!"

Well, Dad could have said yes. He could have said no. He could have said, "I'll leave it up to you."

He said, "Well, I tell you what, son. I'm leaving it up to you," and went right back to reading his paper. (As I said, I hated that answer.)

I walked back to my room, and I'm thinking, *Man alive. What am I going to do?* All I could think about was Six Flags and the rotten time I had. I also thought about my grandmother, who was eighty-five years old at the time. And we only got to see her once a year, at best.

I picked up the phone and called my friend. I said, "Dave, you may not understand this, but I'm not going. There's no way in the world that I can go down there for a week and feel as bad as I did at Six Flags. We are going on family vacation, and I'm going to spend a week with my Nana."

"You're kidding, right?" Dave sure didn't understand.

Anyway, we went up to Pennsylvania for the Fourth of July week and spent a wonderful time with my grandmother. It was great.

A few more weeks went by, and school was about to start back. Right before school opened, my friend, Terry, called me back.

He said, "Caz, you sure did miss a great time at that end-of-the-year party. It was rocking. We are doing a back-to-school party just to celebrate a great summer. It's going to be at my house again. It's going to be awesome. You don't want to miss it."

I said, "I don't think I'm gonna be able to go."

Terry said, "Well, just ask."

"OK. I'll ask." (I was a glutton for punishment.)

So sure enough, I walked into the den where my dad was reading the paper, of course. "Hey, Dad."

"Yes, sir?" he said, pulling the paper down. "What do you need, son?"

"Well, you remember that guy, Terry?"

"Yep."

"Dad, you remember that party I missed?"

"Yep."

"Well, Terry is having another party. A going-back-to-school party. He wanted to know if I could come because I missed the other party."

Well, you know the drill. My dad could have said yes. He could have said no. He could have said, "I'll leave it up to you." Dad pulled his paper down, looked at me right square in the eye with a little grin, and said, "Sure, son, you can go." The paper went right back up, and he started reading again. That was it.

Somewhat puzzled, I said, "What'd you say?"

"Sure, you can go."

I pulled a chair up in front of my father and said, "Dad, you have to explain something to me because I don't get it."

He said, "What are you talking about?"

"Look, I wanted to go to Six Flags on a Sunday, and you said 'I'm leaving it up to you.' Then I wanted to go to Terry's party, and you said, 'No.' Then I wanted to go to the beach with Dave and you said, 'I'm leaving it up to you.' Now I want to go to the same kind of party that you said no to, and now you are saying yes. You are not making any sense to me. I need some answers here. How are you making your decisions?"

"Son, do you really want to know?"

"Yes, sir, I do."

"OK, son," he explained. "When you wanted to go to Six Flags on a Sunday, you knew it wasn't right because of our agreement. But if you decided to go anyway, there wasn't going to be any way that you were going to be hurt. You were going to be in a safe place and in good hands with Skip's family. When you decided to go, you made a poor choice. I was letting out the line for you to see how you would respond, but you didn't choose wisely.

"When you asked me to let you go to a party that you and I both knew might have some questionable things going on, I needed to make that decision for you. I was afraid that if you went to that party, you would make some bad choices that could have long-lasting ramifications.

"As the summer went along, a friend of yours asked you if you would like to go to the beach—a great opportunity, a wonderful thing to do. Again, I knew you were in good hands, so I decided to leave it up to you. You said no because you knew it was best to stay with your first commitment. That decision made me feel like I could trust you to make good choices. So when you asked me about going to this party, I know there are going to be some things going on there that may not be good. But you've shown me you know how to make good choices. You are not going to be able to avoid these things all of your life. So I'm going to let you go to that party, but I'm also trusting you to make good decisions while you are there. I hope you don't let me down."

I said, "I won't, Dad." And there was no way I would have. He trusted me, and he told me so.

My dad looked for opportunities to "grow me." Essentially, he said, "I'm going to give him the opportunity to make the right choice. If he makes the wrong choice, I have to let him go. It's not like he's sticking his hand on a stove. He's not going to get hurt. But he knows what is right and what's wrong. Let's see what he does with it."

It wasn't until I told this story to someone else that I realized *I* needed to be looking for those "grow me" opportunities with my own children.

My Daughter's "Twelveteen" Lesson in Trustworthiness

When my oldest daughter, Lauren, was "twelveteen," she had an opportunity to stay home and spend the night with a friend instead of going down to see my mother for her birthday. (My dad has now passed away.) My mother is seventy-nine years old, she is in good health, and we think she is going to be with us for a long time. But Lauren is getting older and busier all the time.

Although she gets to spend the night with friends all the time, she still asked me, "Daddy, do I have to go this weekend, or can I stay here and spend the night?"

I will be honest with you; my first reaction was, "Yes, you have to go with us this weekend, there's no choice. It's MomMom's birthday." But right before it came out of my mouth, I said, "You know what? I think I am going to leave it up to you."

That wasn't what she wanted to hear. "I just want you to tell me what to do," she said. "I will do whatever you tell me."

I repeated, "No, I think I need to leave that up to you."

She, unlike me, made the right choice the first time.

Also about this same time, she had been asking me, "Daddy, I want my AOL to be teen AOL. I don't want to be on the kids AOL; I want to go to the teen AOL because I want to be able to do instant messenger with all my friends."

Some of Lauren's friends had been on teen AOL for a long time. However, I want to be careful where my children go, what they do, and what they are exposed to through the Internet. Until I was sure that she wasn't going to be going into chat rooms and different kinds of places she didn't need to be, I wouldn't let her move up to the teen level. I think she must have asked me at least fifty times if I would change her access to a different age group with our private code, and at least fifty times I had said no.

The night we got back from visiting my mom in Atlanta, I was in my bedroom getting unpacked. Lauren came running in just like she did weekly, and she said, "Dad, there's a bunch of my friends online. Can I move up to the teenage thing tonight?"

Without blinking an eye, I said, "Sure."

She just left and ran out of the room. Suddenly, she turned around and said, "What did you say?"

I said, "Sure you can!"

"Really?"

"Yes!"

"Why 'yes' after all those times you said 'no'?" she asked.

I explained, "Because last weekend you made a tough choice, but you made the right choice. You showed me that I could trust you. So, I'm going to let you move up to that next level because I do trust you. And my hopes and prayers are that you won't let me down."

She ran across the room, jumped up in my arms, put her arms around my neck, and said, "Daddy, I never will."

I pray that is true. I'm sure that if she is like any other little girl, she will make mistakes in her life. But, I guarantee you one thing—she thinks about that promise every day. Everywhere she goes with her friends she is aware that I trust her to make good decisions. And she thinks about it in advance.

Just a couple of weeks ago, Lauren had an opportunity to go to the beach with her friends. They are at that age where a lot of them are talking about parties and the different places they are going to go and different things they are going to do. They see girls in the ninth, tenth, and eleventh grades who are going to these parties, and they are drinking and making poor choices. Lauren and her friends talk about these things when it is dark and they don't have to look each other in the eye. They ask probing questions of each other, like "I wonder if we are going to drink when we get the chance? I wonder if we are going to do that when we get to that age?"

Finally, one of them said to Lauren, "What are you going to do?"

She said, "Well, no! Of course I'm not going to do that! I thought we made that decision a long time ago."

She challenged her friends to make decisions before it was too late. She's finding out that some of them haven't made certain decisions yet. They think they can wait until the moment arises, but as you know by now, "When the opportunity arises, it's too late to prepare."

As parents, we must look for teaching opportunities that will help our children create trustworthiness.

We have to prepare our children, as hard as it is, by letting that rope out a little bit at a time. When they make mistakes, reel them in; but when they do it right, keep letting it out. Equip and empower so that when the time comes, you are ready to let go of your *winners!*

CHAPTER 19
Pick Your Battles

We are preparing our children to be trusted. When your daughter or your son is at the age she or he can walk out of your house alone and you know you can trust him or her, that's all you can do. You have about thirteen years to make your child trustworthy. If you don't think that you are a vital part of molding and making that happen, you will let valuable opportunities slip between your fingers. You have to take advantage of every opportunity you see to build that trust.

It is also important in every situation not to react judgmentally when your children are working through a mistake. Leslie is teaching me to be better about this. As a parent, be ready to pick your battles so that, in the end, you win the war.

Take ear piercing, for instance. When I was a teenager, I am sure if I had ever walked into the house with a pierced ear, I would have been looking for another place to live! My military father would have never put up with that. As a result, I'm not very tolerant of the idea of boys with pierced ears either.

My wife, however, reminds me that it's a fad, and my daughter might come home someday with a young man who has a pierced ear. If I fight that battle (ear piercing), will it help win the war (finding the right mate for my daughter)? These are things about which parents have to think. Male ear piercing is a fad that will probably disappear someday. What's more, there will be other fads. The important thing is the winner on the inside, not the fads that come and go.

My father, because he was a military man, detested long hair. Even so, he bit his lip and swallowed as I allowed my hair to grow longer in the '70s or '80s. My brother did the same. Our father knew that long hair was a fad. He reserved his energy for the battles that were necessary to win the war.

You have to pick your battles. There are certain situations with your children when you have to ask yourself, "Is this the end of the world? Can they learn something from this? What are they going to learn from this situation?" If they are learning or teaching lessons in the game of life, then it is probably a positive thing in the long run as long as the lesson is not going to hurt them or cause lifelong detriment to their personal being.

Just be sure to remember that when some guy comes to pick up your daughter and he is wearing an earring! Then send me a note and remind *me* that it will be OK!

CHAPTER 20
Purity Is Important

Many years ago Leslie and I had the opportunity to lead a group of twelve girls on a discipleship retreat. At the time, these girls were twelve and thirteen years old.

The theme of the weekend was sexual purity. Lack of morality is running rampant among our young people in this country. Because it's a very private act, sexual activity is an easy thing to hide. It's not like drinking or smoking or doing something that you do in crowds. Even "good kids" get caught up in this premarital sex thing because they think they truly love the person they are dating. Kids get a lot of pressure from their friends to become sexually active before they are married. The scary thing is, it is happening to students at younger and younger ages.

When we began our meeting with the discipleship group, I brought with me a single red rose. I talked about that rose and the fact that God made it. I commented how it was a seed at one time and then grew to be a very pretty flower. It had all of its leaves in a bud, and then it finally bloomed. It smelled wonderful, it was soft, and it was gorgeous.

I asked every one of the girls to look at it and think about how amazing it was that God created it. I handed it to the young lady that was sitting next to me, and she smelled it. I said, "Now, feel how soft it is."

She then passed it on, and that beautiful rose went around the circle. Each girl passed it to the next girl, and each held it, smelled its one-of-a-kind aroma, and felt its soft petals against her face. Some even took one petal off and saved it as a reminder of this time.

When they all had touched it, the rose came back to me. I said, "Now I want to give each of you a constant reminder of the fact that God made you as beautiful as He did that rose. I have a gift for you." I reached down behind my chair and pulled out twelve more roses. I laid all of the roses out on the table, including the original rose that everybody had already handled and passed around.

Then I said, "Now, one by one, I would like everyone to pick out a rose to keep."

Each girl came and picked out a rose. Thirteen roses and twelve girls. Can you guess which rose was left? The flower that had been passed all the way around the room was still sitting there on the table. I said, "Why didn't anybody pick this rose?"

Each of those young ladies said in one way or another, "It has already been passed around the room. Everyone has already had their nose in it, and it has its petals missing. I wanted my own brand-new rose."

I then replied, "Each one of you is exactly like that. I want you to think about the man out there whom you are going to spend the rest of your life with. Does he want a rose that has been passed all the way around the room? Or does he want a brand-new fresh rose just like you?

"I know you have a lot of friends who say, 'Hey, have you lost your virginity yet? Are you sleeping with your boyfriend?' They might even tell you that they have and that you should.

"Let me tell you one thing they can never have again that you have. They can never again have the purity you have. At any given moment, you can become just like them, but they can never be like you again. That's the reason they want you to do it so badly—they don't want to be the only one who has messed up. They will feel like they made a right choice if you join them.

"But remember, when you get older and you are shopping for husbands, those men will be looking for someone who is unscathed."

When I tell this story to young men, I say, "Don't think that you are not a rose in the eyes of young women. They don't want guys who have been jumping around from one rose patch to another either." Pure young ladies are looking for young men who are also pure.

I recently decided to give my daughter a "purity ring" as a symbol to her, and to all those who know her, of her commitment. Many refer to this as a "True Love Waits" ring. I thought for a long time about what kind of ring to give her. Then I had an idea!

As you know, most ladies take on their husband's last name when they get married and then use their maiden name as a middle initial. I decided to buy Lauren a silver signature ring for her wedding finger with the initials L __ M on it. The large initial representing her last name was left blank because she is saving that spot—and herself—for her husband. Lauren loves her ring. It tells her story—her testimony—everywhere she goes!

CHAPTER 21

Children Need to Know What Is Real

My dad was a great encourager. As I was growing up, he often put challenges out there to help me realize my potential. It is important for parents to teach children to do their best. In school if your best is making B's, then that's great. But if your best is making B's, then you don't need to be making C's. If your best is making C's, then you don't need to be making D's. If you have the ability to make A's, then you need to make A's.

To encourage kids to meet their potential, parents sometimes must offer incentives. Take the story of Shane, for instance. Like most teenage boys Shane wanted a car badly. He went to his dad and said, "Dad, I really would like to have a car when I am sixteen."

Dad replied, "I tell you what, son. If you will do three things, we will go out and get you a car on your sixteenth birthday."

"Great, Dad, what do I need to do?"

"Number one, you need to get straight A's in school this semester."

"All right, I am up for that."

"Number two, you must cut that long, nasty hair that is hanging over your collar. Number three, you have to read your Bible every single day."

"You've got a deal, Dad," said Shane.

For the next three months Shane studied hard, staying after school, going after extra credit, spending time with the teacher. Shane got his report card back, and sure enough, for the first time in his life, Shane had straight A's right down the line.

Shane also had been reading a chapter in his Bible every day. He wrote the date by each chapter and even took notes to prove that he had read it.

Shane went to his Dad on his sixteenth birthday and said, "Dad, time to get that car."

Dad said, "All right. Let's see that report card first, son." Shane pulled out the report card showing straight A's.

"Son, I am so proud of you. I knew that you had it in you."

Shane stuck his chest out. "Well, you know, Dad, I have to admit, I didn't think I had it in me. But it was pretty exciting, and I'm glad that I did it."

He then said, "Now look right here, Dad. For the last three months, I have been reading the Bible. I started here and went all the way through—every day—a chapter a day. And you know what? I am going to keep doing this. This is great stuff. Now, let's go get that car!"

"Hold on there, buddy. We got one more little thing here. What about you getting that hair cut?" Dad asked.

"Well, let me just tell you about something, Dad. I have been reading the Bible on a daily basis, and I've got some things to show you. It says right here that even Jesus had long hair."

To which Dad replied, "That's right, son. And He *walked* everywhere He went."

Aside from a little humor, Shane's story is about incentives. If there are things we want our children to do, there are things we can do to encourage them. We can often help them build character by giving them an incentive to reach a goal. Roger Breelan, longtime director of Christian music group "Truth," says that he told all of his children if they got a full scholarship in anything, he would buy them a brand-new car of their choice. All four children got full scholarships, and despite the cost of the new cars, he probably saved hundreds of thousands of dollars on school tuition.

Some of my favorite times with my own children have been while challenging them to solve their problems, to figure out how to meet the need before them. It's just a system of goal and reward. Following are some stories that demonstrate how I've worked with my children on problem solving.

Never Trust a Snake!

My children's elementary school has an annual Colonial Day. One year they asked me to come dressed as an American Indian. Part of my assignment was to tell Indian stories. I went to a good friend and former staff colleague, Dr. Kirk Neely, who knows a great deal about American Indian culture, and he shared a story with me. I decided it was very applicable.

On Colonial Day, I sat in front of group after group of fifth graders at Pine Street School. Dressed in authentic-looking Indian chief garb, I told them this story.

> In a lot of Indian tribes when a child turns twelve, he gets an Indian name. The Indian name is based on a challenge given to that child by the Indian chief. The Indian chief decides the

challenge the child has to take on in order to prove his manhood.

On one particular child's twelfth birthday, he stood before the chief, and the chief said, "Your challenge is to go to the top of that mountain, spend the night, find your own food, prove you have been to the top, and come home."

Well, just the journey to the top of the mountain took a couple of days. Although the weather at the bottom of the mountain had been hot, as this child's journey continued, he realized it was getting colder and colder. The mountain was actually quite cold at the top. Sometimes, animals worked their way to the top during the day without realizing how cold it gets at night. Unable to get back down the mountain, the animals sometimes died. Well, this little boy was a pretty smart kid, so he had packed extra clothes. He finally got all the way to the top of the mountain and spent the night there.

In the morning, as he was looking for some sort of proof that he had made it all the way to the top, he saw a rattlesnake. The rattlesnake was almost frozen stiff because it was so cold. As the tale goes, the rattlesnake looked at the boy and said, "Put me in your shirt and make me warm next to your body and take me to the bottom of the mountain."

But the boy replied, "I can't do that. You will bite me, and then I will die."

The snake promised, "I won't bite you. You are going to save my life. Put me inside of your coat and make me warm because if you leave me here, I will die. If you will take me and put me inside of your coat and take me to the bottom of the mountain, I promise I won't harm you."

The boy picked up the very stiff rattlesnake, put him inside of his coat next to his body, and began his journey back home. The closer and closer the boy got to the bottom of the mountain, the warmer and warmer the snake got. When the boy's body heat returned the snake back to its normal temperature, the boy opened his shirt to take the snake out. Suddenly, the snake bit him.

Just as the boy was about to die, he looked at the snake and said, "You broke your promise. You bit me."

The rattlesnake looked at the young boy and said, "You knew what I was when you picked me up."

This story teaches a lesson that applies to many of our children's circumstances. I want to remind them of that story when they are staring in the eyes of a "rattlesnake" on a date or at school or any place they go. Often young people think, *Well, maybe this time it won't hurt me. Maybe this time it won't kill me. Maybe this time, I won't get in trouble.*

But the point is, they know what it is when they pick it up. They know what is right and wrong. They know what are potentially life-changing mistakes. This story—like many others— gives children something to hold onto when they are faced with difficult decisions.

A Deep Foundation Is Important

When Lauren was in five-year-old kindergarten, crews were building the very first high-rise building in Spartanburg, South Carolina, right across from the church where our children were in preschool. Lauren's preschool teacher used to bring the children out to the site where they were building to watch what was going on. They couldn't wait to see the building going up.

The crew had cleared off the area and were getting ready to start building. Cranes began by digging a big hole. After that hole was dug, they took all of the cranes and literally set them down in the hole. Then the cranes started to dig a deeper hole in the ground.

One day the crane operator climbed up out of the hole. His name was Mr. Chuck, and all the children knew his name. When Mr. Chuck came up out of the hole, the children were excited to see him.

The teacher said, "Does anybody have any questions for Mr. Chuck?"

Immediately Lauren raised her hand. "Mr. Chuck, we came here to see a big old building that is going up. Why are you digging such a big hole?"

Mr. Chuck shared a lot of wisdom in his next comment. He said something that has run over and over in my mind for many years. Mr. Chuck told the class, "If you want to go up high, then you got to dig deep."

In other words, a deep foundation is important. I have applied that idea to my own life, and I want my children to apply it to their lives. If we want to grow closer to the Lord, we have got to go deep in our prayer time, we have got to go deep in our quiet time, we have got to go deep into our relationships with our own children. If we want to go up in our character, up in our integrity, up in our relationships with other people, up in our relationship with the Lord, we must dig deep into God's Word.

I think you would be absolutely amazed at the number of people whose relationships with their children is extremely superficial because they don't understand, or want to understand, each other. They don't realize it's because they don't listen to their children. Listening, however, is one major way we dig that deep foundation so necessary in our job as parents.

One thing that I encourage you to do if at all possible is to pick up your children after school. It's fine to carpool in the morning on the way to school, but pick up your children on the way home from school every chance you get. Then when they get in the car and close the door, just listen. Look for the longest route home and give them plenty of time to talk. You will be amazed at what happens. My wife will not miss picking up our children for anything. They talk and talk and talk as soon as they climb in the car. My wife tries to avoid having other children in the car because our children sometimes won't talk about their day around others. And if they get all the way home and get in the house, it's over and done with by then. They will call a friend or keep it to themselves.

That ride from school to home is valuable time. As your children talk to you, you must be careful not to immediately react in a negative manner or say, "Let me tell you what you need to do." Just listen and let them talk and talk. Don't drop your jaw over something you hear. If you go deep in your relationship with your children, they will ask you for advice when they need it. They will ask you what you think. But if you act shocked and amazed or say how ridiculous something is, it will be the last time they will tell you anything. You just have to listen and let them get it all out there. Then that after-school ride will become a treasured time for you and your children.

Be Who You Are

Another story I've shared with my children is the story about Barry Bremman. This man actually got his kicks out of being an imposter. In 1979, he showed up at the Grammy Awards dressed as an actress on the show *Hill Street Blues*. When that lady's name was announced as best actress, even though the lady was there, sitting in the back, Barry jumped up and went across the platform, accepting the award for this lady. Of course, it didn't take long for officials to catch him because the real lady came down to accept the award just moments later.

Not long after that, Barry Bremman put on a practice uniform for the Kansas City Kings basketball team. He showed up at the NBA All-Star game and warmed up with the team. Nobody stopped him. That same year, in similar fashion, he took batting practice at the Major League All-Star game. No one had any idea who he was, but he went unnoticed until almost game time.

In 1980, he walked onto the field at the World Series dressed as an umpire. He greeted players, shaking hands, and saying, "How ya doing? Good to see you." When all the umpires gathered at home plate right before the ball game, the head umpire counted: "One, two, three, four . . . who are you?" Only then did they kick Barry Bremman out of the park!

That same year, Barry Bremman played three holes of golf at a practice round of the U.S. Open with Curtis Strange before anyone realized who he was, and, believe it or not, he watched an entire Dallas Cowboys football game from the sidelines dressed as a Dallas Cowboys cheerleader!

He even showed up at the 1981 Super Bowl dressed as the San Diego chicken—and got in the game!

In each one of those situations, Barry Bremman tried to convince others that he was someone that he wasn't. He tried to take a shortcut to success. And in every situation, he ended up getting kicked out, pushed to the back of the line, and thrown out! Now there are other ways to be successful than by playing for the Kansas City Kings or in the Super Bowl. Our children need to understand that to be a success, they need to be *themselves*—who God created them to be.

When I told my children that story about Barry Bremman, the lack of character and integrity on the part of this man amazed them. The story, and our long talk about it, helped them see the importance of being who you are as opposed to being who you think other people want you to be.

Our children are winners just as they are. It is up to us, as parents, to help draw it out!

CHAPTER 22

Conflict Is
a Teachable Moment

Your child's conflicts are character's teachable moments. Think about that for just a second.

Your children are going to have conflicts in their lives. In a basketball game there are conflicts. Whenever there are ten players on one side of the court and ten players on the other side of the court, twenty parents over here and twenty parents over there, forty grandparents over here and forty grandparents over there, and a referee in the middle, conflict is going to occur.

The question is, when you have conflict, what are you going to do with it? How are you going to use it as a teachable moment or as a ministry opportunity? You need to be close to your children; you need to be a part of who they are and where they are.

I've told many stories about my dad sitting in his chair and reading the paper—but that was when I was in my teens. By that point in our lives, we could sit and talk about things. When children are young, however, parents must be a part of the action!

Dr. James Dobson says that you can't parent from a Lazy-Boy recliner. For example, you can't say to your child, "Go get in the bathtub," and if they don't move, say it again, "Go get in the bathtub." And if they still don't move, you finally *yell*, "Go get in the bathtub!" The message you give to that child is, "He doesn't really want me to take a bath until he yells for me to go take a bath."

What needs to happen is that you say, "You need to go get in the bath at the next commercial" or ". . . when you finish that game" or ". . . when the timer goes off in five minutes." And if they are still sitting there ten minutes later, there needs to be consequences for not going and getting in the bathtub *the first time* you said to. Consequences are different for every child, but there needs to be consequences for not going and getting in the bathtub the first time.

Matthew 12:34 says, "Out of the overflow of the heart the mouth speaks." I love that verse. I often have to reflect on it when conflicts arise in our home.

Everybody has disagreements. The question is, how are you going to deal with these conflicts? As a Christian, what makes the way you deal with conflict different from the way somebody who doesn't know the Lord deals with conflict? Sometimes the easiest thing to do seems to be to get upset and yell at somebody.

Consider the illustration of a cup. If I've got a cup of tea in my hand, and somebody walks up to me and bumps me, what's going to come out? Tea. If I have coffee in my cup, and somebody walks up to me and bumps me, what is going to come out? Coffee. If it is water or milk, the outcome is the same— whatever is in there is what's going to come out.

Matthew 12:34 says that the same is true in our lives—what is in our hearts eventually comes out. We all know that everything is not going to be perfect in our lives. We've all experienced conflict in the past, and we are all going to experience conflict in the future. The question is, when you get bumped in the game of life, what is going to come out of your mouth? The answer is what is in your heart. Will it be the love of Jesus, who lives in you? Or will it be anger from somewhere in your past? Maybe it is stress at work. Those things will come out. Whatever is in our hearts at the moment is what is going to come out.

I have three daughters. If conflict arises, sometimes before I ever say a word, they fill up with tears of emotion just because they dislike conflict. That's a teaching moment. They have to learn from those situations. If it is true that a child's conflict is his or her character's teachable moment, then that child can learn something from it. It is an opportunity to bring out the winner in that child. Remember our definition of a winner is: somebody who is learning or teaching lessons in the game of life. If you can teach a child something through a mistake or even through a conflict, then that child's a winner.

A lot of parents say, "You don't have any idea how many conflicts my child comes up with." Well, if that is so, then he can be winning a lot if he's learning something from those teachable moments.

Probably one of the greatest things we can do for our children is to encourage them to memorize Scripture. I still benefit from the different things my Mom made me memorize: Psalm 1, Proverbs 3:5–6, John 3:16, just to name a few.

In the back of this book are thirteen foundational Scripture verses. These are life-changing verses that I encourage you to begin teaching to your children. There are only thirteen; that's only one a month—with one extra! Have your child read each verse a hundred times (but not at one sitting). If your child reads these verses over the course of a month, a year, two years, or three years, he or she will memorize them without even realizing it. The Bible says, "I have hidden your word in my heart that I might not sin against you" (Psalm 119:11).

The more he or she reads these verses, the more they become a part of who your child is and what he or she does. (Now that's an engram!) As your child applies these lessons of Scriptures in their lives, the winner in your child begins to come out.

CHAPTER 23

Clear Direction

Children need clear direction in order to develop strong character.

Have you ever taken a moment to observe children and their parents in public? I can't even count the number of times I have seen a child get in trouble with his or her parents in a mall or grocery store or at the library. In most cases, the problem developed mainly because the child didn't understand what was expected of him. The child didn't have clear directions from the parents.

Providing clear direction for a two-year-old child is completely different from directing an eight-year-old. And it is different for an eight-year-old as compared to a fourteen-year-old. The older your child gets, the more she will be able to comprehend.

I remember many exciting times with our young children when they were learning to take direction. If we said to them, "Go get me your tennis shoes," they did it! But if we had said, "Go to your room and get your tennis shoes and socks and a diaper," it would have been much more difficult for them. There would have been too many things in their path to distract them. They might have come back with a Frisbee, or they might not have come back at all.

That is certainly not something for which a child should be punished. It is up to us as parents to understand the capabilities of a child's mind. Children need clear direction in order to understand exactly what you want them to do.

My favorite example of this (told by permission) involved Keighlee, my middle child, when she was in three-year-old pre-school at the church at which I was on staff.

Keighlee had clear direction from her mother at home. The first thing we do at our house when we come through the door is take our shoes off and leave them by the door so that we don't drag mud through the house.

When Keighlee went to preschool, however, she took that habit with her. (She actually took it with her wherever she went.) As soon as she got in the door at preschool, she took off her socks and shoes and left them by the door. This became a little frustrating for the teachers because whenever they wanted to go outside for recess, they had to wait for Keighlee to get her socks and shoes back on.

The teachers tried to change Keighlee's "engram." When she got there every morning, her teachers would say, "Don't take your socks and shoes off. We are going to go outside in a little while."

Well, it didn't matter how hard they tried, five or ten minutes later, Keighlee would be over in the corner taking her socks and shoes off and putting them by the door. Finally, the teacher called me and said, "Listen, I hate to bother you with this, but every time Keighlee comes in the door, the first thing she does is take her socks and shoes off. It is really becoming a problem because now it is not just Keighlee taking her socks and shoes off; she has everyone else taking their socks and shoes off too. It takes us forever to get all of those socks and shoes back on the children."

I realized I needed to step in and do something. I sat down with Keighlee that night, put her in my lap, and had her look me right in the eyes. I said, "Keighlee."

She said, "Yes, sir?"

"You know that when you come home, Mommy and Daddy always like for you to take your socks and shoes off and put them by the door."

"Yes, sir."

"When you go to school, you don't have to take off your socks and shoes. As a matter of fact, I want you to keep your socks and shoes on all day. Do you understand?"

"Yes, sir."

"When I take you to school tomorrow and I drop you off at preschool, are you going to keep your socks and shoes on?"

"Yes, sir."

"You promise you are going to leave your socks and shoes on all day?"

"Yes, sir," she said in that cute little voice.

"I want you to make sure you keep your socks and shoes on. Do you understand?"

"Yes, sir."

In the car the next morning: "Keighlee, when you get to school today, are you going to keep your socks and shoes on?"

"Yes, sir!"

"Good girl, darlin'." I was so proud of myself. I was changing her engram.

We got out of the car, went inside, and just as we were about to get inside the door, I said, "Now, Keighlee, what are you going to do?"

Keighlee whispered, "I am going to keep my socks and shoes on, Daddy."

"That's a good girl, Kiki."

I watched her walk inside, hesitate just a second by the door, and then proceed to find some friends to play with. I was so proud. I called the teacher over and said, "I just want you to know that I had a long talk with Keighlee last night. We chatted a little bit about the socks and shoes problem. She's got a clear understanding. We talked this morning; she's still got it. Keighlee went in just a minute ago and went to the play area with her shoes still on. I don't think you are going to have any problems at all. If you do, I want you to call me because I told her not to take off her socks and shoes. I am pretty convinced she won't, but if she does, I'd like to come down and deal with it myself."

"OK," the teacher said, "I will give you a call if I need to."

As I finished my conversation with the teacher, I stuck my head in to say good-bye to Keighlee. When I walked in and said, "Good-bye, Keighlee," she was standing on top of the little orange slide with her socks and shoes on, just like I told her to—and that was all! She had *nothing* else on! My little girl was stark naked—except for her shoes and socks, of course.

With the biggest smile you have ever seen, she said, "Bye, Daddy! I got my socks and shoes on!"

"That's a good girl, Keighlee! Now you need to come with me out here in the hallway for a minute. And bring your clothes!" It was evident that she needed a little more clear direction.

That was a classic moment in the McCaslin memory bank. Keighlee was going to get comfortable by taking something off when she walked in the door of her preschool, but she knew for sure it wouldn't be her socks and shoes. The good news was that that time she didn't impact all of the rest of the children!

Clear direction is *very* important.

Sometimes our children get mixed messages. Mom says one thing; Dad says another. When the children go to Grandma's, they get yet another message—usually something like "anything goes!"

How many times have you heard about grandparents who let their grandchildren do a whole lot more than their parents ever will? Sometimes my wife and I go out of town, and one of the grandmothers comes to take care of the children. It usually takes us a good two or three weeks to get our children back in line after their "relaxed" time with Grandma!

Sometimes, it only takes a few hours with Grandma to impact a child. One of the funniest things that ever happened in our family was when Mari Caroline was just learning to talk. She was at that "parrot" stage of her language development.

Every time we go home to visit my mother, even though she loves all of her children and grandchildren, I am my momma's baby boy. I am the youngest of four children and even though she can't wait to see all of the grandchildren, whenever I walk in the door, the first thing she says when she sees me is, "There's my boy!"

She puts her arms around me and kisses me and then she takes the grandchildren and off they go! She has always greeted me that way every time I see her. "There's my boy!" She still does that today.

My mother had a tremendous impact on Mari Caroline. One time when we got home from "MomMom's" and resumed our daily routine, Mari Caroline listened for me to come in the door. Every time she heard my keys rattle, I would hear those little feet pattering around the corner and she would jump up in my arms and say, "There's my boy!"

Rarely over the next year did she call me "Daddy."

I certainly never told her anything different. It was classic! Her sisters began to influence her, and she now calls me "Daddy." Those are treasured moments and they flee too fast. Although a little bit of "anything goes" from grandparents won't hurt your child, all-in-all you want to make sure that you, as parents, are giving clear directions that are appropriate to the age of your child. Clear direction every day will diffuse many arguments before they ever get started. What's more, it will surely bring out the winner in your child.

CHAPTER 24

Actions Are Character on Public Display

Your child's attitude is a great measuring stick because your child's attitude is his or her character on public display. In fact, the same truth applies even as we grow older. A person's attitude reflects his or her character. You can pick up on a lot of things about people, including your children, by simply observing the attitude by which they carry themselves. Of course, all of us have times when we are frustrated, but these frustrations provide opportunity for our character to grow.

Has your child ever spent the night in someone else's home and the host parents say, "Your child is so well-behaved. Your child has the best manners." Your response might initially be, "Did anybody else spend the night over there? Is that my child you are talking about?" Even though you might not always see the behaviors at home, it is a blessing to have someone else compliment your child.

You know at least some of the teaching you have been doing and your examples really have been making a difference. Attitude at home is important too. We work on it in our home on a daily basis. One of my favorite Bible verses is Galatians 2:20: "I have been crucified with Christ and I no longer live, but Christ lives in me. The life I live in the body, I live by faith in the Son of God, who loved me and gave himself for me."

Perhaps you are familiar with the WWJD bracelets so many people wear—What Would Jesus Do? Recently, I heard someone make the following comment: "You know, it should be more than 'What Would Jesus Do?'—that would be merely *acting out* what you think Jesus would do." In fact, Galatians 2:20 tells us not to act out what you think that Jesus would do, but to *let Jesus do it through you.* Let Jesus' attitude live through you. Let Jesus' attitude and actions take place through you. Submit yourself to the point where you actually allow Him to do His work through you. It becomes more than action; it's an attitude. By decreasing yourself, it's no longer you but *Christ* who lives in you.

For me, attitude was something that was also taught to me by the different coaches for whom I played. One particular football coach gathered the team together at the beginning of each season and taught us how to spell *attitude*. At every practice and game, we huddled up, and instead of saying "Go, team!" or "Big D," we would shout, "One, two, three! A-T-T-I-T-U-D-E!"

Coach would ask, "How we gonna win this ball game? How we gonna do it?"

And we'd answer, "A-T-T-I-T-U-D-E!"

"We're gonna win this ball game. How are we gonna do it?"

"A-T-T-I-T-U-D-E!"

"We are gonna play the best we can, right? How are we gonna do it?"

"A-T-T-I-T-U-D-E!"

The answer to everything was attitude. And I don't think it really hit me until much later that if we want to bring out the winner in an individual, we have to have a good attitude. And if we're teaching or learning lessons in the game of life, then we're winning; and if we are winning, we will have a great attitude. There's no question in my mind that every child is a winner. I don't mean every child *can be,* or *will be,* a winner. I mean that every child *is* a winner. It's simply our responsibility as adults to draw it out of our kids.

That football coach had a tremendous impact on my life and on the lives of my teammates by drawing a positive attitude out of every player on the team. We were not permitted to have a bad attitude. We couldn't hang our heads about a pass that we dropped or a tackle that we missed or even a game that we lost. Our attitude had to reflect a positive light in everything we did. By taking on a positive attitude, we always had to look for the good in everything. This is a lesson we can teach our children at any age.

Don't Miss the Circus!

Ken Smith, former chaplain of the Florida State Seminoles, tells the story of a young boy named Willie.

Willie lived in an old country town and dreamed of going to the circus one day. Willie had always heard about the tigers and the elephants, and he wanted to go to the circus. Willie asked his dad if he could go to the circus if it ever came to town.

His dad said, "Well, son, if it ever comes to town and you have enough money, then you can go to the circus."

Well, sure enough, about three weeks later they started posting signs all over town that the circus was coming. It would cost $2.25 to get in. Willie went home and opened up his piggybank. He counted his money, and he had $1.15.

Willie went to his dad and said, "Daddy, the circus is coming to town in about three weeks. I've got to have enough money to go. I'm short, and I need some money."

"Well," Dad said, "I will give you some extra chores to earn some money, and if you get them all done, then you can go to the circus."

The day before the circus came to town, Willie finished up his final chores, and his daddy gave him the rest of the money he needed. Willie woke up on Saturday morning and asked his daddy if he could go ahead and go into town to watch the circus.

Dad said, "Son, the circus isn't going to be in town for another five or six hours."

"I know," Willie said, "but I don't want to miss a thing." So he ran down to the town. He was there four or five hours waiting on the curb for the circus to come. The street started filling up with people. Crowds were coming from every direction. The shoulders of the road were roped off and packed full. The band could be heard playing in the distance. Spectators could almost feel the ground begin to shake as the elephants were coming. The parade was on its way. It was so exciting!

Willie could barely contain himself as the parade came into view. The first thing through was a marching band playing incredible circus music as they walked down the middle of the street. Right behind were the clowns, juggling and riding unicycles. Then the big cages came through. In the first cages were the tigers and the lions. Then came the cages with the gorillas and monkeys. Finally, Willie saw the thing he had been waiting for—the elephants. They trudged along, swinging their trunks in front and swishing their tales behind. There must have been eight or ten of them connected trunk-to-tail, hanging onto each other.

The crowd cheered and yelled for nearly an hour as the parade went by. When it got completely to the end, there was a guy riding on a big unicycle with a big tray full of popcorn. He stopped at different people to see if they wanted popcorn.

The man came right up to Willie, pulled out a bag of popcorn, and said, "Would you like a bag of popcorn, son?"

"Yes, sir."

He handed Willie the bag of popcorn and said, "That will be $2.25."

Willie reached in his pocket, took out his $2.25, handed it to the man, and the biggest smile came on Willie's face that you have ever seen.

Willie ran all the way home, thinking about the incredible circus. He went straight up to his dad and said, "Dad, you wouldn't believe the circus. It was absolutely awesome. There was a band and lions and tigers and elephants and monkeys. And they all went by in these big cages, and the elephants came by, and the clowns were hilarious. Then the last guy who came through gave me free popcorn, and I gave him my $2.25 and came home."

Dad asked, "Why are you here so early?"

"Because it was over."

"Son, you didn't see the circus. All you saw was the parade. You have just been watching the parade go by. They took your money for the popcorn."

The reason I tell that story is because this life is nothing but a parade. If you know Jesus Christ when you die, you will go to be with Him in heaven for eternity—and that is where the circus really begins.

Learning or teaching lessons in the game of life is what draws out the winner in each of us, and the most important lesson we can learn is how to become a child of God. This life in which we now live is nothing more than a parade. The circus is when we get home, when we get to be with Jesus Christ and spend eternity with Him.

All too often we forget why we are really doing what we are doing. Why is it that we are here? We get so wrapped up in today, or maybe even yesterday, that we forget about tomorrow.

God created all of us. The Bible says that before you were in the womb, God knew you. And God doesn't make mistakes. He doesn't make losers. He created us for two reasons: to have fellowship with Him and to tell others about Him.

Summary

I think it is important to actually write down "My child *Lauren* is a winner. My child *Keighlee* is a winner. My child *Mari Caroline* is a winner." The truth of the matter is, if you realize that your child *is* a winner, you look at your child differently. You don't say, "He doesn't do what the neighbor's child does," or "He can't keep up with some of his friends." You say, "My child *is* a winner, and I'm going to do everything I can to bring out the winner in my child." When you openly acknowledge that fact, it changes the way you treat your children. It changes attitudes. It even changes the way that they learn. They understand that they *are* winners.

Take just a minute and do a quick inventory. **Can you say with confidence:**

* *I* am a winner! [ ] yes! [ ] no   (If you answer no, re-read the book!)

* My child _____ is a winner!

* My child _____ is a winner!

* My child _____ is a winner!

* My child _____ is a winner!

* My child _____ is a winner!

Remind yourself and each of your children that everyone is a winner!

Thirteen Foundational Scripture Verses

Matthew 12:34b: "'For out of the overflow of the heart the mouth speaks.'"

Proverbs 3:5–6: "Trust in the LORD with all your heart and lean not on your own understanding; in all your ways acknowledge him, and he will make your paths straight."

1 Corinthians 10:13: "No temptation has seized you except what is common to man. And God is faithful; he will not let you be tempted beyond what you can bear. But when you are tempted, he will also provide a way out so that you can stand up under it."

Galatians 2:20: "I have been crucified with Christ and I no longer live, but Christ lives in me. The life I live in the body, I live by faith in the Son of God, who loved me and gave himself for me."

John 3:30: "'He must become greater; I must become less.'"

Colossians 3:17: "And whatever you do, whether in word or deed, do it all in the name of the Lord Jesus, giving thanks to God the Father through him."

Philippians 4:13: "I can do everything through him who gives me strength."

Psalm 1:1: "Blessed is the man who does not walk in the counsel of the wicked or stand in the way of sinners or sit in the seat of mockers."

Romans 3:23: "For all have sinned and fall short of the glory of God."

Romans 6:23: "For the wages of sin is death, but the gift of God is eternal life in Christ Jesus our Lord."

Romans 10:9-10: "That if you confess with your mouth, 'Jesus is Lord,' and believe in your heart that God raised him from the dead, you will be saved. For it is with your heart that you believe and are justified, and it is with your mouth that you confess and are saved."

1 John 1:9: "If we confess our sins, he is faithful and just and will forgive us our sins and purify us from all unrighteousness."

1 Chronicles 4:10: "Jabez cried out to the God of Israel, 'Oh, that you would bless me and enlarge my territory! Let your hand be with me, and keep me from harm so that I will be free from pain.' And God granted his request."